The Re-birth
of a
Born-Again Christian

The Re-birth
of a
Born-Again Christian

— A Memoir —

For Eve Howie with love and wonderful memories

JAMES A. SANDERS

Jim
April 2017

CASCADE *Books* · Eugene, Oregon

THE RE-BIRTH OF A BORN-AGAIN CHRISTIAN
A Memoir

Cascade Books
An Imprint of Wipf and Stock Publishers
199 W. 8th Ave., Suite 3
Eugene, OR 97401

www.wipfandstock.com

PAPERBACK ISBN: 978-1-5326-0706-6
HARDCOVER ISBN: 978-1-5326-0780-0
EBOOK ISBN: 978-1-5326-0707-3

Cataloging-in-Publication data:

Names: Sanders, James A., 1927-, author.

Title: The re-birth of a born-again Christian : a memoir / James A. Sanders.

Description: Eugene, OR: Cascade Books, 2017.

Identifiers: ISBN: 978-1-5326-0706-6 (paperback) | ISBN: 978-1-5326-0780-0 (hardcover) | ISBN: 978-1-5326-0707-3 (ebook).

Subjects: Racism—United States | United States—Race relations.

Classification: E185.615 S26 2017 (print) | E185.615 (ebook).

Manufactured in the U.S.A.   04/06/17

"The Betrayal of Evangelicalism" first appeared in *Bulletin of the Colgate Rochester Crozer Divinity School* (Summer 2012) 8–13, 18–22. Used with permission.

–Contents–

— prologue —

T he evangelical movement in the USA was an early nineteenth-century issue of the so-called Second Great Awakening in the context of America's expansionist policies of Manifest Destiny and occupying the vast land west of the Alleghenies. It satisfied the tremendous need of those who dared venture into the then-unknown (to those of European descent) fertile territories inhabited by native Americans who bravely tried to defend their centuries-old homeland. Being Christian, the invaders felt the need either to convert the "savages" or to massacre them—the way their reading of the Bible indicated the ancient Israelites had done in invading and occupying ancient Canaan. They felt totally justified by their reading of the Bible, just as the Dutch, Spanish and Portugese had felt justified in conquering and suppressing the native Americans in both the Northern and Southern "new-world" continents in the name of the Roman Catholic Church and the general Christian mission to convert the whole world.

The Christian movement in moving westward with the "pioneers" in both continents provided needed mandates for the stealing of native lands, making and breaking meaningless treaties, and slaughtering or repressing the first Americans. Those who dared to venture west of the Alleghenies were all from European Christian lands who often had escaped various forms of persecution there and sought fresh beginnings in America. Among these were the Irish and Scotch-Irish but there were numerous others as well, especially Germans and Scandinavians, from north European lands. For the most part they were lower-class and lacking in forms of liberal education—that is, thinking beyond "tribal" values. In fact, their intense needs were greatly satisfied by the anti-intellectual tendencies of those who had ventured forth to live where there were as yet no schools and certainly no colleges or universities. They imported left-wing (at the time) Protestant Reformation doctrines that emphasized the worth and responsibility of the individual. The left-wing Protestants of the European Reformation had nowhere to go for any form of higher education except those founded and

1

run by Roman Catholics that they eschewed on principle. That lack had produced various forms of anti-intellectual tendencies in Europe that were readily transported to the American frontier.

Protestantism from its beginnings with Martin Luther in the early sixteenth century was a product of the Renaissance emphasis on individual worth and importance. They could thence no longer adhere to the Catholic doctrine that salvation was "in the Church only" but focused on the individual's acceptance of redemption by the grace of God in Christ apart from The Church. Each individual could accept that grace without regard to Church doctrine and responsibility. This developed into the cherished belief of (at the time) left-wing Protestant teaching that the individual needed but "accept the Lord Jesus Christ as one's personal savior"—a huge reduction in requirements to becoming "Christian."

The Reformation had been a product of the Renaissance in Europe that in itself was the "re-birth" of the Hellenization process that slowly came to a halt after Constantine's Christianization of the Roman Empire. The Hellenization process had begun following Alexander the Great's policies in the fourth century BCE toward the tribes and peoples he conquered. Alexander mimicked the earlier policies of Cyrus of Persia's whereby those he conquered who submitted to his rule were granted status and power sufficient to thrive—as long as they submitted to the monarch's overarching rule. This created throughout first the Persian Empire and then Alexander's a process of amalgamation of cultures that extended thereafter under Roman rule whereby the worth and responsibility of the individual no matter his/her origin gained force despite the continuing collective needs of each culture to assert itself.

The potent combination of individualism and anti-intellectualism provided the energy and stamina of the pioneers in their drive west of the Alleghenies and then west of the Mississippi River. Little churches were eventually established in hamlets and villages along the way that re-assured the conviction of the pioneers that they were doing God's work, along with the satisfaction of their own supposed needs for acquisition of land and a life of what they viewed as individual freedom to take what they needed when they needed it without regard to the native Americans they dispossessed along the way. After all, they were godless heathen, weren't they? The same Scotch-Irish, German, and other north European immigrants that populated the areas South of the Ohio River not only dispossessed the native Americans of The South but also purchased other humans forcibly imported from Africa to do the back-breaking labor that would eventually enrich some whites to become fabulously wealthy. Because of the rank individualism cherished by poor whites even they fell into the trap of bigotry sanctioned not explicitly but deeply effective against those they massacred and dehumanized for the sake of the American economy and its manifest destiny. Because of the drive to satisfy the needs of the north European immigrants the humanity, and not just the needs, of native Americans and the forcibly imported Africans, have been forcibly denied.[1]

Ever since the conquest of Constantine, and his early fourth-century CE Christianizing of the ancient Roman Empire, Christians have frequently dehumanized those that got in the way of the missionizing of Christianity wherever it has gone. Because the youth in "Christian societies" are not taught the centuries of cruelty and inhumanity by Christians in their efforts to spread the Gospel to all peoples, most people in the West have no idea why current non-Christians in the Orient have such low opinions of Christianity in most of its forms. After Constantine, when Christians became dominant in the Roman Empire, they turned around and did to Jews what the earlier Romans had done to them. To the non-committed Christianity has a miserable record of dehumanizing those who are different. Therefore, it is little wonder that the pioneers who settled the vast territories west of the Alleghenies had little compunction in stealing and dehumanizing those different from them.

What follows is the personal account of a born-again white Southerner who grew up in a totally Apartheid culture that he did not question until he heard in college of a form of Christianity that questioned Southern culture and eventually the racism of America at large. Those who introduced him to "liberal" Christianity were themselves originally from Texas and Mississippi but had earlier learned to take seriously the teachings of Jesus and the Prophets before him. It was a conversion every bit as powerful as the experience he'd had as a child a decade earlier in a Pentacostal tent revival. He'd always cherished the earlier experience as that of a born-again Christian.[2] And even after learning of the revolutionary teachings of Jesus he could never deny the deep-felt earlier experience. He put the two together in his soul and became a follower of the deeply radical teachings of the Jew from the Galilee.[3]

1. See the powerful statement of America and racism in Jim Wallis's *America's Original Sin: Racism, White Privilege and the Bridge to a New America* (Grand Rapids: Brazos, 2016)

2. See the dedication to my *God Has A Story Too* (1979; reprinted, Eugene, OR: Wipf & Stock, 2000): "For Sisters Agnes and Iris and my sister Nell, women who told me the tomb was empty, and for Ruth and Joe Brown Love, who told me my head need not be."

3. Gary Wills in his *Head and Heart: American Christianities* (New York: Penguin, 2007), in which he aptly shows the origins and differences between the highly individualized understanding of the faith by fundamentalists and evangelicals and the more

Critical reading of the Bible, especially the Gospels and the letters of Paul, showed him how radical Jesus' teachings were over against the repressive rule of the Roman Empire of the time. Reading the Bible critically is to recognize that reading a text, any text, requires two basic factors: the text and the reader. To read the Bible critically as a literary product of a particular people of the Ancient Near-East and Eastern Mediterranean area is to engage in the excitement of recovering the original meanings as nearly as possible of its authors. The Jew or Christian can then responsibly believe that God used the ancient cultural idioms and metaphors in which the Bible is expressed and then also believe that God can use current human cultural idioms and metaphors to engage in the search for the truth about ourselves in our short four-millenium period of existence and search for ultimate meanings of human being.

To take a biblical text seriously is to study it within the ancient Near Eastern or eastern Mediterranean context in which it was conceived and found expression in an ancient language, specifically the Hebrew and Aramaic texts of the First Testament (Old Testament) and the koiné Greek of the New Testament. The serious reader wants to know as nearly as possible what the original authors and editors meant and intended in composing the text. To read the Bible only as "The Word of God," even if one knows some Hebrew and/or Greek, usually means ignoring the original cultural contexts in which a text was composed but to read it in the context of what the current reader thinks he/she knows of the Bible—usually a scrapbook Bible of texts chosen to convey a chosen message with the concomitant belief that the Bible is totally harmonious and inerrant and therefore supports in toto the scrap-book of collected familiar passages.

But a text, any text, is but scribbles on leather, parchment, papyrus, paper, or more recently on a cyber-screen, until it is engaged by a reader. Inevitably the reader, whoever it is, is a product of a human culture, just as the text addressed was a product itself of a human culture. The reader brings to the text the presumptions and presuppositions learned in the culture of which s/he is a product. Reading Scripture critically means setting aside one's pre-conceived ideas about what the Bible is or means but instead reading it in the context of the historical and cultural situations of the era in which the various parts were written. It taught the author that reading the Bible literally was to deny its true meaning both in antiquity and

---

traditional expressions that understand that the Bible is but one base of authority for the church along with reason, tradition and experience. Fathers Philip and Daniel Berrigan, whom the writer knew personally and admired in the days of turmoil in New York City in the late 1960s early 1970s, lived lives of a combination of personal experience and the teachings of Jesus.

today. Reading the Bible critically opens up the biblical text to meanings well beyond tribal interpretations and beginning to walk the path of the monotheizing process the Bible describes and prescribes. He learned to read the Bible honestly and seriously, but not literally. In fact he learned that one must read the Bible with three H's: honesty, humility, and humor.

Reading the Bible with *honesty* means breaking out of the hermeneutic circle one perpetuates when one reads the Bible expecting it to say what one was taught in *schul*, church, or Sunday school it should say.

Reading it with *humility* means identifying in reading a biblical passage with those whom the prophets and Jesus addressed and admitting that we are as sinful as they had been. This in effect means using dynamic analogy in reading with humility. Being a "Christian" does not mean one is exempt from identifying with the so-called "bad guys" of biblical history.

And reading it with *humor* means taking God a little more seriously and ourselves a little less seriously each time one reads a passage of Scripture.

Jesus' teachings riled the good religious folk of his time (read "us") and got him crucified for proclaiming the reign of God as superior to that of the greatest Empire of all time, and he did so without "firing a shot" or supporting any kind of violence.[4] It should by dynamic analogy disturb us and the great country in which we live. As Luther and Calvin both taught, salvation comes only through God's judgments of us and not through our denouncing others and abusing the Bible to do so.

4. See Elisabeth Schüssler Fiorenza, *The Power of the Word: Scripture and the Rhetoric of Empire* (Minneapolis: Fortress, 2007); and Schüssler Fiorenza, *Jesus and the Politics of Interpretation* (New York: Continuum, 2011).

—chapter 1—

LUCERNE PLACE

I was born into and raised in a railroad, working-class, blue-collar neighborhood in Old South Memphis. Lucerne Place, where we lived, is a one-block street between Third Street on the west and Latham Avenue on the east. It was a white enclave at the time located adjacent to a black neighborhood with Latham as the invisible iron-curtain between the two.

I was the eighth of eight children of Robert E. and Susie B. Sanders. Dad was a steam locomotive engineer who worked for forty-four years for the Nashville, Chattanooga and St. Louis (NC&StL) Railroad. They had both come to Memphis from Fayette County, just east of Shelby County where Memphis is county seat. The NC&StL in the late nineteenth century created the little town of Laconia near where they both grew up. I was born in November 1927 at the height of the roaring twenties only a couple of years before the crash that led to the Great Depression. This meant that I was almost five years old when Franklin Delano Roosevelt became president and my father's hero until his death.[1]

We children had no reason to question the Apartheid culture that divided Lucerne Place from our neighbors to the east. They were basically not permitted to cross the great divide, nor did anybody from our side cross Latham. There was a psychological wall dividing the two cultures. Exceptions were that blacks from down there crossed the line daily to come up to the back doors of the various houses on Lucerne to do the cleaning, cooking, yard work, and the like. The black "aunties" that came up to "help" our

1. James A. Sanders, "Memories of My Father: Robert E. Sanders," *Dixie Flyer: The Official Newsletter of the NC&StL Preservation Society* 12/4 (November 2014) 14–15; Sanders, "Memories of Steam: Growing Up on the NC&StL," *The Dixie Flyer* 13/2 (Summer 2015) 1, 8–9.

own mother we called Lulu and Katie. Katie's husband and son did some of the yard work around the house, but it was Lulu we Sanders knew best. Lulu was my "mammie" when I was a baby, and she was our mother's savior at the height of the terrible flu epidemic of 1917. I wasn't born yet, but I often heard our mother tell the story of how she would have died if Lulu had not gotten in bed with her to put "her big black back" against our mother's back at a crucial moment in Mom's illness. Lulu and Katie, especially Lulu, were members of our family, or so I was told—except that they entered the house only through the back door and left after a hard day's work through the same door. It would have been impossible to imagine that a black person, even Lulu, would show up on our front porch.

I'll never forget the moment when a black man from down in the "bottoms" below Latham dared to walk up Lucerne and speak to my parents in front of our house. It was such a momentous occasion that a small crowd (of whites, of course) gathered to see what was going on. The black gentleman was wearing his Sunday-go-to-meeting suit and tie. Daddy was at home between runs on the railroad. I'm sure the black man didn't dare come up on the porch to knock on the front door. Momma was always home. She never left the house without one of the family with her, usually one of my sisters who accompanied her to get the Third Street street-car to go downtown to Bry's Department Story on rare occasions. I didn't know the black man's name, but to this day I marvel at the guts it took him to cross the barrier that day to stand on the sidewalk in front of our house. Momma came out with Daddy to see what was afoot. The gentleman had come up to complain to my parents that some of us white boys had taken to "playing little cars" in the dirt mound under his front porch down in the "bottoms." I recall, and can never forget, that he spoke with great deference to my parents to request that we children quit playing under his porch without his permission. My mother turned to me to ask if it was so, and I lied. I told the lie that has lived with my soul ever since. I said, "No'm" to my mother (being translated "No, ma'am"). I knew that I was lying, and I was certainly hurting inside. Mother then slapped me a stinging blow across my face. That slap was the first and only time my mother ever hit me, but it has to this day a lingering sting nothing can soothe. My parents knew that that gentleman would not have had the courage to come up to our house (albeit just the sidewalk out front) if what he said was not true.

I sulked out of the scene and made my way to the back of our home where I sat on the back stoop and cried my heart out. It hurt all the more because I knew Mom was right and I deserved the rebuke. The crowd must have dispersed and the black man returned home, but I didn't see that. What I saw was my father come join me on that back stoop and put his arms around me. He quietly said, "You lied, didn't you, son?" I nodded "Yessir" through my sobs. And then my father said the words that I'll never forget. He didn't forgive me. He and I both knew I was wrong on the two counts: playing under the man's porch down where I should not have, and denying what he said was true. No, he didn't forgive me. What he said was, "Muddy didn't mean to hurt you, son." I shall never forget those words. She did hurt me, and I knew that I deserved the slap, but I had never in my life ever imagined that my mother would strike me. She never had and she never did thereafter. Neither did my father, for that matter. All he'd ever had to do with us kids was look disapprovingly at us and we melted. But there he was sitting on the back stoop with his arms around me to comfort me in my guilt. My parents, mind you, were not all of a sudden integrationists, not at all. They, on the contrary, were firming up the wall that both we kids and the black gentleman had dared violate, he justly and we unjustly.

I have often wished in later years that I had found a way to tell my Mother how much her rebuke meant to me as the years went by. I guess as a kid I was glad that the incident was never brought up again. I didn't say what I have since wished I had. That moment was seminal in my life. I still wasn't ready to question Apartheid, but I think it taught me to respect another person's space no matter how humble and poor it was. I don't know exactly how we white boys thought up the idea of playing little cars under that porch down there. It was the first house just below Latham and easy to reach, and we must have thought it'd be OK to use that enticing mound of dirt under that porch to make little roads and run our little cars on them. Nonetheless, it was across the border. It was beyond the pale. It was forbidden territory. They could come up to our turf to clean and work for us, but we couldn't go down there. Yet we kids did that once, and the black gentleman also did from his side just that once. The lesson my parents taught me that day was not just that I was not supposed to cross that line, but that I was supposed to respect another's life space, their Lebensraum. It didn't bring me to question Jim Crowism yet, but it stuck with me deeply that I in effect desecrated another person's home by disrespecting where he lived.

There was another occasion that lifted every so slightly the "iron curtain" that separated our lives in those days. It was a balmly June evening in 1938 and we kids on Lucerne were out playing after supper when all of a sudden we heard noises we had never in our lives heard before. They were coming from down in the Bottoms, and they were frightening to us. Normally one never heard a thing from down there, but that evening the shouting was almost blood-curdling to our little white ears. Nearly everyone by then had a radio no matter how small. It was still an amazing invention to most of us, and most of us white families had at least one radio in our homes. It still was not of great interest to us kids; I mean Orphan Annie, Flash Gordon, and Amos and Andy had their fifteen minute shows on the radio in the hour or so after we got home from school each day, but nothing in the evening caught our attention. I suppose none of us kids at that point was interested in boxing. Anyway we had no idea why such a frightening clamor interrupted our play. We knew it came from "down there" but that was all we knew that night. It was not until I asked my brother Welch later that evening after I'd returned home if he knew why there was such a raucous noise from the Bottoms. He said that an American boxer, Joe Louis, who was "a Nigger" had beaten a German boxer by the name of Max Schmeling. Welch didn't say anything demeaning that I remember at the time, but it was clear that it was something new in our lives that was beginning to happen and I could sense that he was concerned. I don't recall hearing anything about Jesse Owens winning gold Medals at the Olympics in Germany in 1935, and I don't remember any noise emanating from the Bottoms when he did. If there was I didn't hear it. But the black folks' reaction to Joe Louis' flooring Max Schmeling by a decisive first-round knock-out in 1938 tore through my Jim Crow soul as nothing ever had done before. I actually felt fear, and rightly so.

Memphis and Shelby County in those days had a political boss, E. H. Crump. We were like the rest of the South in those days, a part of the solidly Democratic South. The Crump political machine ran smoothly and nearly everybody benefitted. It was powerful. One of the first things Crump did that benefitted everybody was turning the utilities companies into a city-owned and operated Light, Gas and Water facility. Members of my family have worked for the Memphis LG&W. My father told me that before the facility was created the privately owned electric company often left the street lights on well into the morning, but that after the LG&W was restructured as a municipal utility street lights were turned off soon after dawn and did not come back on until dusk. In 1950 Memphis passed at Crump's behest an ordinance against black smoke emitting more than a few minutes from any locomotive serving the area. Memphis had nine railroads either terminating in Union Station, like my father's and the Southern Railway, or stopping in Grand Central Station like the Illinois Central, the Missouri Pacific, and the Rock Island. A couple of locomotives were photographed in fraction of the new ordinance and top officers of each of those Roads were put in jail for a day. Crump's word was law that even powerful railroad officials daren't ignore.

Each neighborhood in Memphis had a ward healer and we on Lucerne Place knew exactly who that was, Mr. Cook on the corner of Lucerne and Latham. If there was any problem all we had to do was have a visit with Mr.

Cook and it was fixed. Crump was politically astute enough that he would see to it that blacks in Shelby Country had a ton of coal centrally located in all their neighborhoods—and that they had the right to vote, a rarity in the South in those days. They may not have known what the issues were that concerned Mr. Crump, but they were told clearly how to mark their ballots and they knew exactly where Mr. Crump had left them coal enough to keep warm in the cold of winter. Elections in Tennessee thus pretty much went the way Crump wanted because of the huge number of ballots cast in Shelby County. One story that made the rounds after the Second World War had started was about two blacks, one of whom was worried that Mr. Hitler would come and take over the country. The other responded that they didn't have anything to worry about because Mr. Crump wouldn't let Mr. Hitler come over in the first place. What did not seem to bother them or much of anybody else was that the reason Crump worked it so that blacks could vote (when most of the South had poll taxes and other barriers to blacks' voting) was to make sure the Republicans, who in those days were the Party of Civil Rights, didn't win any local or Tennessee state election.

All us Sanders kids went to Lauderdale Grammar School several blocks from Lucerne Place and to South Side High School a bit further away but definitely still in white-occupied Memphis. We kids never questioned the fact that there were no black kids in school with us. I never learned where schools for black kids were located if there were any in our part of town. Apartheid was imbedded in the culture and we never (at least in those days) asked why. We knew in walking to school or in riding our bikes where it was OK to go and where not; we just knew. But the way to get to school, or to church or scout troup meetings, for white kids in our immediate neighborhood, was to walk or ride our bikes along Latham over to Walker Street that we took in those days to get to any of those venues. At the beginning of the Depression Daddy sold our Model A Ford so that was no longer an option for getting about. The only "wheels" we had were our bikes and public transportation. The street-cars that ran along Third Street (parallel to Latham) cost 7 cents during all of my childhood and the Depression, and blacks sat in the back, of course. The Joy Theatre up on McLemore Avenue cost 10 cents Saturday afternoons where we went to see Flash Gordon and Tom Mix beat "the bad guys," but there were no seats for blacks at all. I'll never forget when admission at the Joy started costing 11 cents. It was a shock. What was the world coming to?

Another occasion on which I lied, afraid of being caught in the Apartheid trap, was once when I was riding an electric city trolley coach down town. I was probably about eleven or twelve years old. Our bus driver, purposefully or not, hit a black man's car when the bus driver pulled away from the curb. The black man was caught in a vise of traffic and was not at fault. The bus driver was wrong to pull away from the curb with a car directly in his path. I could see that the driver knew the car was on his side but he pulled out anyway. The bus was stopped by a patrolman, who investigated the incident while we bus riders waited out the delay. The patrolman was thorough in his investigation and asked each of us on the bus if we'd seen what happened. I had seen it all and knew the bus driver was at fault, but I told the patrolman that I did not see what happened. A black gentleman on the bus gave me a hard look that I shall never forget. I knew I was wrong, but I also knew that I was expected to side with the white bus driver, which I did. That incident is also seared into my soul. I felt guilty and still do that I did not witness for the black man driving the car hit by the bus. But I feel that this incident with the occasion of the black gentleman coming up Lucerne Place to complain to my parents were occasions in which my very soul was being prepared to question what at the time I didn't even know how to question but was easy to lie about. Was something in me being prepared for battles yet to come? I don't know, but I do know that these are memories indelibly seared into my being. Even at that age I knew that as a white boy I would get away with the lie while the black man driving the car would clearly lose his case, in part because I lied.

There was one anomaly on Latham, and that was a Pullman porter and his family. His beautiful home on Latham was on the south edge of the Bottom but up on Latham itself. He not only owned one of the more beautiful homes in the whole area (including ours) he also owned what we kids called the "big field" on our side of Latham. The "big field," was the grazing area for his horse. We kids were allowed to play in the "little field" directly back of the houses on our side of Lucerne Place but not in the "big field." Our parents never told us who owned that field but they did say that the horse belonged to the gentleman who lived in the beautiful house on the other side of Latham. We rarely saw the gentleman or his family, but I always admired his home, especially the beautiful garden out front. I guess, as a Pullman porter, he was an early example of what the black middle-class would look like.

— chapter 2 —

BORN AGAIN

Among my happiest memories of childhood were my annual visits with my Aunt Sallie and Uncle Joe Perry at Fairview, their plantation out about two miles from Laconia, the tiny hamlet seven miles east of Sommerville, the county seat of Fayette County, founded in the nineteenth century by the NC&StL Railroad. It was a flagstop for the Road in those days (1930s and 1940s) so that I was able to use a Railroad pass issued to my Dad to travel by train from Union Station in Memphis to Laconia, and back. As a kid I loved everything about my summers at Fairview, not only living and playing on the farm but riding the train by myself to get there and back. Uncle Joe would meet me at the train when I went out there and then take me back to Laconia to return home. He taught me how to use his big white handkerchief to flag the train down to catch it to return home. I liked my stays out there so much that once when I got home I cried after my mother asked me how much I enjoyed my stay at Aunt Sallie's. She at first thought I cried because I'd had a bad experience, but I blurted out that I was unhappy I couldn't stay longer. I think that hurt her a bit, but she didn't say anything.

Once while I was out there they drove me to Sommerville to meet my father's train coming from Memphis when he pulled up to the coal shute near the station. Dad motioned to Uncle Joe to hand me up to him in the cab. Dad put me on his lap for the short ride to the water spout. I'll never in my life forget the sensations I experienced riding in the cab of my father's steam locomotive—even that short distance. The choo-choo noise was rather muted in comparison with the terrible hissing noise of the brake. I asked my father later at home in Memphis how he could stand it, it was so loud. He said some of the fellows went deaf because of it. But he never did.

It was at Fairview that I learned how a farm operated in the Deep South in those days. Again I didn't question how the blacks were treated because I was growing up in Southern culture and it didn't occur to me to question what everybody (white, that is) accepted as normal. Uncle Joe accumulated real wealth as the owner of the plantation. While my parents were out there once, probably for a family funeral, my father and Uncle Joe were chatting in his study when Uncle Joe got out a bag of Bull Durham and some papers and commenced to roll himself a cigarette. Dad asked him why he rolled his own when he probably could buy the company that sold the tobacco. Uncle Joe, in his deep bass voice, said, "Well, Bob, I know that when I'm a-rolling 'em I'm not a-smoking 'em." Uncle Joe not only grew acre upon acre of cotton, he also owned a herd of Whiteface Herford cattle. He also put in acres of corn and lespedeza to feed the cattle, but not as much as cotton, of course. Cotton was the cash crop. He also raised sorghum that Aunt Sallie and her "help" made into delicious syrup.

When I say that Uncle Joe grew these crops I mean, of course, that the tenant farmers or sharecroppers did. Uncle Joe spent most of his time sitting in his big swivel chair with his feet up on the desk reading. Uncle Joe had twelve black families who lived on the farm in shacks he provided them scattered about the plantation. I heard him once tell Aunt Sallie that so-and-so (the name of one of the tenants) asked one early spring if he could start planting cotton in March. Uncle Joe indicated that he liked the spunk of the man but he told him it was his gamble if he did so and the weather turned bad on him. When I was there later in the spring one year I got to see the cotton plants blooming. One morning a whole field of cotton would be solid blue and the next morning solid white.

It was a beautiful sight, but, of course, I had no idea at the time of the arrangement Uncle Joe had with his tenant farmers. I heard later that they generally could make as much as $100 a year working cotton for Uncle Joe. My uncle, of course, claimed most of the yield of a field of cotton anywhere on his farm, but the black tenants could some years make as much as $100 for the year's labor. During the Great Depression that was not bad compared to what some blacks in Memphis earned, but they owed as much as half of it back to Uncle Joe. Uncle Joe laid in supplies of food in the basement of the big house that he distributed on set days each winter to the black tenants who would show up at the back porch door to get what they needed for a while—a side of bacon, a bag of flour, a bag of corn meal, a tub of lard, and so on. At least that is what I saw he gave out to each of them as they came to the door. Whatever he gave each he marked in a ledger against each name. Then when cotton-picking time in the fall came and each tenant got his due for the year, each tenant had to reimburse Uncle Joe for what he had supplied them earlier in the year. I don't know how much they owed but it was probably half or more of whatever they earned that year. Sharecropping was worse in ways than slavery had been because the "massa" back then was obliged to feed whatever "stock" he owned, including his slaves.

I was never taught or told about the "Black Codes" enacted in Southern states in 1865–66 that restricted the freedom of former slaves. Using old tactics such as vagrancy laws, convict leasing, and debts, white Southerners effectively nullified the effect of the Thirteenth Amendment. These tactics had been used earlier to keep native Americans in servitude in the West long after slavery had been made illegal by the same amendment. Formal slavery was replaced by multiple forms of informal labor coercion, indebtedness, and enslavement that were extremely difficult to track or eradicate. I had no idea, of course, that Uncle Joe's practice of keeping his sharecroppers indebted to him had gone back so far in the South since the Civil War.

What I observed was that emancipation by Mr. Lincoln nearly a century earlier ended up after Reconstruction meaning very little indeed. When the Union troops went back North and Reconstruction was rescinded by the South-dominated white Congress, Jim Crow local laws threw the blacks back into situations that were about the same as slavery had been, or worse. They didn't buy and sell them outright or flog them, or separate black families from their children, they instead lynched them for the least insubordination to keep them in subjugation. As I grew and became aware of their plight I again accepted it as part of the culture that no one questioned, including white preachers of the Gospel. I knew that most Protestant churches where I grew up had "South" or "Southern" in their titles. When I was a kid I went with a neighbor family to Calvary Methodist Episcopal Church South. Friends went to a Southern Baptist Church. I later learned that these names came about in the nineteenth century when the issue of slavery caused most Protestant churches to split into Northern and Southern branches. But again we did not question such names until we learned American history outside the South.

The treatment of blacks when I grew up was not questioned even by "good Christians" in the South just as "good Germans" were not questioning what Hitler was doing to Jews, Gypsies and homosexuals in the same time period in Europe. Southern Christian deacons and elders did not drag blacks off to gas ovens, they just squelched their humanity, denied them any dignity whatever, and kept them in shameful, inhuman poverty. The school system throughout the South was separate and anything but equal. An educated black, slave or free, was a danger in the minds of white Southerners.

In Memphis my mother and I worshipped at Calvary Methodist Church and I never once heard a voice raised to question the culture in which we all were nurtured even though we heard the Gospels read every Sunday and supposedly studied the teachings of Jesus in Sunday School.[1] Why? Nearly every church in the South was "evangelical" and focused on the individual's salvation, born again accepting "the Lord Jesus Christ as Lord and Savior." Social ethics was either never mentioned or was openly denounced. I heard even recently a white evangelist loudly proclaim that social ethics was of the devil. Of course it is, because it would question the whole system on which Apartheid society is based. How could we object to what Hitler was doing even if we had known about the Holocaust? What Hitler did to Jews good Christians in the South were doing to blacks if they dared step out of the lines Jim Crow laws had drawn. Oh, we didn't pack them off to concentration camps to be gassed, but we kept them so subjugated both on farms and in cities in the South that there was little difference in terms of what one would expect of "good Christians." Just like before the Civil War the economy of the South has always been built squarely on the backs and the pain of black folk.

I literally grew up in Calvary Methodist Episcopal Church South on McLemore Avenue—a totally white part of the city in those days. When I wasn't at school I was at church. I faithfully went to Sunday School, Scouts, choir practice, Vacation Bible School and any other churchly activity designed for white children and youth. We learned Bible lessons and sang some of the wonderful hymns whose words should have raised questions in our minds, but did not. We had "Brotherhood Sunday" every February in church but not even that raised questions about what whites were doing to blacks. We sponsored missionary activity in African nations and raised money to feed the poor abroad, but we did less than nothing for the Afro-Americans in our own city. Individuals and families would "take care of the help" with the occasional sack of flour or cornmeal. We were told that they were happy with their lives and were best left alone to enjoy them. What was made abundantly clear was that "they were best left alone." I recalled later in life when I studied the Civil War and its causes that we didn't even question the word "South" attached to the church name. I to this day have no idea where the schools for black kids were in those days, either grammar or high school. Neighborhoods were so structured that we did not have to see blacks unless they came to the back door or rode in the back seats of street cars and buses. The official policy was that education was "separate but equal." The

1. See Robert W. Lynn and Elliott Wright, *The Big Little School: Two Hundred Years of the Sunday School* (New York: Harper & Row, 1971).

unofficial policy was that education was separate but very unequal. As in the days of slavery one didn't want Negroes to become educated or they might not stay in "their place."

It never occurred to me to ask how blacks managed to travel about in our wonderful, "free country." Much later I learned how unfree it was for people of color, where they could stop overnight while driving, or where they could stop to eat. In fact it wasn't until I read an article in the *Smithsonian Magazine* that a guide book for black travelers began to be published in 1937 that provided information for the black traveler listing hotels, taverns, garages, night-clubs, restaurants, service stations, barber shops, beauty parlors, etc., where they could safely and comfortably stay or shop without being harassed or humiliated. It was titled "The Negro Motorist Green-Book" compiled periodically by Mr. Victor H. Green, and did not cease publication until 1967, three years after Congress passed the Civil Rights Act. There are in fact, according to the Smithsonian article, "Green Book sites" still in existence for places in Las Vegas and Los Angeles compiled and published in a blog online. Much of the focus is to list places "in the middle of nowhere" where it is much more dangerous for people to go.[2] This brings to mind a similar publication that a student brought to my attention years ago that listed bars, baths, hotels, and other venues where gays are welcome and can feel at home without being harrassed.

There was to be no fraternizing whatever after the age of five or six. Up to that age little white kids could play with little black kids in acceptable circumstances, but after a certain moment, usually when we started going to school, that abruptly stopped. Again we kids didn't know to question the culture; we were nurtured in it. It was a part of us and no one, no matter how born-again, or "saintly," questioned it. We learned to call the blacks who worked in our homes "Uncle" and "Auntie." To us at the time that seemed warm and family-like and not at all condescending as I later learned it was to blacks. We even thought they loved us given all we personally did for them and they did for us, like Lulu's saving my mother's life in the flu epidemic. It was not until later that I learned how condescending nearly all our relations to blacks were and how much more truly Christian "our blacks" were than we ever even thought to be.

When I was six years old, my sister Nell took me to a Pentacostal service on Third Street where the first Holiday Inn in the country was later constructed. The service was held in a tent in the depths of the Depression a few years before they built a little clap-board church on the same spot. They

2. Jacinda Townsend, "Driving While Black," *The Smithsonian Magazine* (April 2016) 52–53.

were having a "revival" meeting. Anyone who lived in the South in those days knew what a revival meeting meant. Calvary Church in co-operation with the Disciples of Christ Church and the Southern Presbyterian Church, all on McLemore Avenue, held revival services every night that lasted two weeks each summer. Services would be held in one of the churches one week and a different one the next and so on for three weeks. Out in Fayette County the same denominational churches co-operated each summer by each holding revival meetings two weeks each in sequence so that they didn't conflict, and so that the (white) farmer-families in the area had something social to do every summer night during "laying by" time for six weeks running. Cotton farmers, white and black, all knew the meaning of "laying by," the period after hoeing out the weeds and before cotton picking started, when the plants were best left alone to mature.

My sister Nell took me to the tent meeting up on Third Street near our home that night. I think I was cover for her to have a date during the service because I didn't see her after she seated me on a bench. Nell once told me she never had a problem having a date whenever she wanted one. She also told me that there were times later in life when she knew she lived in "a state of grace." Sisters Iris and Agnes were holding the revival meetings for two weeks during the summer. Sister DuClos, a local lady, always sat alone in a wheelchair in front of the first row of benches and often would "speak in tongues" when the Spirit moved her. Sister Agnes preached that night and Sister Iris strummed the guitar and led the congregation in singing.

I noticed when I entered the tent that there were brown, wrapping paper strips hanging all around the pulpit like vertical bars of a jail. Sister Agnes' Scripture passage that night was from Acts chapter 16. Paul and Silas had been thrown in jail in Philippi for preaching the Gospel, but while they were praying and singing hymns "suddenly there was a great earthquake so that the foundations of the prison were shaken and all the doors were opened and everyone's fetters were loosened." At that point in the sermon Sister Agnes rolled up her King James soft-leather-bound Bible and swung it around her head so that those brown paper strips were dramatically torn and fell fluttering to the floor around her.

Sitting out in the congregation on one of the two-by-four wooden benches that served as pews the little six-year-old laid his head on the bench in front of him and raised his hand. That was usually a signal to an usher to bring the person forward to the front to kneel to be "prayed through to salvation." The usher in my area of the tent must have seen how small I was and just left me be. But I had to do something, so I took the little tin sheriff's badge my mother and sister had bought me that day, unclasped it from my shirt and put it on the dirt floor of the tent and crushed it under my foot.

In my young mind, I distinctly recall, I was laying down my trophy and sacrificing it to Jesus—not only for saving Paul and Silas from that awful jail; I was convinced that though the earthquake had occurred long ago in Philippi, the prison bars broke that night in Memphis.

Though this memoir is about how racism and bigotry are home-grown American "values" that are closely associated with white evangelical Christianity, I need to make clear my life-long appreciation of the personal experience I had in the tent meeting that night in Memphis long ago. Over thirty years later I published a book of sermons I had preached in the late '60s with the following dedication:

> For Sisters Iris and Agnes and for my Sister Nell, women who
> told me the tomb was empty, and for Ruth and Joe Brown Love
> who told me my head need not be.

That experience would remain with me the rest of my life, and indeed still does. The reference to Ruth and Joe Brown Love will be made clear later.[3]

I didn't notice at the time, of course, but I'm sure there were only whites in that tent meeting. Having grown up in the culture I didn't think anything about it then. And, of course, there were only whites in the churches in Memphis or out in Fayette Country. Blacks had their churches but they were always situated so that whites wouldn't have to see them. Apartheid was everywhere ingrained in the souls of whites and most blacks. I would see this again in South Africa when I was there in 1973 and again in 1989; it felt as though I had been transported back to the Memphis of my youth. If blacks protested in the days of my youth I never heard of it—except perhaps that night in 1938 when Joe Louis floored Max Schmeling. But they were not protesting even then, they were rendering thanks for a glimpse of their humanity despite American denial of it.

The USA did not enter World War II until the Japanese bombed Pearl Harbor on December 7, 1941, and began their war of expansion into the island nations of the Pacific. We at the same time declared war against Germany, which had already conquered most of Europe and destroyed much of London in what they called the Blitzkrieg. For the first year and a half the Western Allies continued to retreat while the Japanese and Germans destroyed hundreds of Allied ships both in the Pacific and the North Atlantic. Most able-bodied young men entered some branch of the armed services and nearly everybody left at home in the US engaged in some aspect of "the war effort." My wife to be, though only sixteen, joined the Civil Air Patrol flying small single-engined aircraft looking for U-boats along the New

---

3. "The Betrayal of Evangelicalism"; see the appendix below.

Jersey shore. I, by contrast, hired on at a toy manufacturing shop in Memphis where I got so bored doing nothing but making holes in toy wheels that I quit after only four days. I then was hired as a clerk in the PX at the First Army Headquarters stationed in the Shelby County Fairgrounds where I did quite well for the summers of 1943 and 1944.

— chapter 3 —

VANDERBILT UNIVERSITY

When it came time to choose a college I decided on Vanderbilt University in Nashville. I had a scholarship I could use wherever I wanted, and after I'd done some searches I figured that Vanderbilt was where I wanted to go. I had made National Honor Society. My sister Nell encouraged me to decide for myself and was obviously happy when I chose a school well away from Memphis. It is about 250 miles from Memphis to Nashville where Vanderbilt is located, and I knew I could use Daddy's railroad passes to go back and forth as schedules indicated. But Nell was pleased with my choice because she rightly figured that if I stayed home and went to a local school I'd be expected to be the principal caregiver for our aging parents. Five of the other seven children lived in or near Memphis; as she saw it I did not have to sacrifice my future just because I was the last child born to our parents. Factored into my thinking was that Vanderbilt was an internationally recognized university whereas none in or around Memphis was at that time. Nell used to tease me about my report cards through the years from grammar through high school. She'd take a look at them and exclaim how boring they were. I loved learning. I loved reading. And I still do. God bless Nell for her support throughout my life and especially when it came time to make that big decision.

The War in Europe was over in June 1945 when I arrived a Sunday afternoon on the Vanderbilt campus and was assigned my lodging in Kissam Hall. I had been told that if I matriculated for summer session I could get deferred from the draft which was still in effect. I would turn eighteen the following November. When the war was over in Europe we all figured it wouldn't take long before the war in the Pacific would also be over. Kissam was one of the oldest buildings on the Vanderbilt campus and looked it.

The outside looked definitely late nineteenth century and on the inside the floor boards creaked and the common bathrooms forbidding to a basically shy seventeen-year-old away from home and the farm for the first time. The rooms in Kissam were arranged so that there were two small bedrooms on either side of a common study room. One look at my home away from home for the following year made me deeply homesick. After unpacking I walked from Kissam over to West End Avenue and caught a bus downtown. I had no idea where I was going but I asked the driver of the first bus that came by where the bus went and he said downtown. I got on determined to get off at the first church I saw open and welcoming. If I had asked someone I could have gone to the big Methodist Church a short distance the other direction on West End, but I was too homesick I guess even to see it. When the bus passed a church downtown that was obviously open and busy I got off and walked straight to the entrance.

It was the First Baptist Church of Nashville. I walked in and found a youth group my age and was heartily welcomed. I soon met my first girl-friend in that group. She was a student at Peabody College near Vanderbilt. I participated in the youth activities of First Baptist for a year including preaching in a tent revival campaign that the church sponsored the following spring. The whole church was totally white, but none of us questioned it. My experiences in First Baptist deepened my Southern roots and did nothing to challenge them. It was totally evangelical, as most Southern Baptist churches were and are, and supported Apartheid.

Back on campus I had a basically good first year for a Vanderbilt freshman. I got a job in the cafeteria in Kissam Hall, first mopping floors, then rising through the ranks finally to become cashier. I continued to work there the three years of my undergraduate days. One incident that has stuck in my memory from working there happened after a group from India came to eat there as guests of the University. Like a good Southern boy, I had become acquainted with and chatted with the black cooks and other workers. They always treated me nicely because they knew to keep their distance but to be nice to the white boy. The black staff noticed that the visitors from India were about as black/brown as they but were treated like whites. One of the workers opened up to me saying with some venom that she didn't understand why the dark-skinned visitors were treated royally while they were discriminated against. It was the first event that would begin to pry my eyes open to a world beyond the Jim Crow South.

I soon became acquainted with a few students who were worshipping at the Belmont Methodist Church near campus. They were the kinds of students that I admired, making top grades with seemingly little effort. One was a student I met in a math class that first summer. His name was Virgil

Mitchel Howie. We soon became fast friends and remained so for six years. Everyone called him Vim. He was pre-med and I was pre-ministerial, both giving us deferred status in the draft. Vim was one of the group who went Sundays to Belmont Methodist Church not far from campus. They invited me to join them but I was involved at First Baptist and stayed there that first year. But they finally persuaded me and I really enjoyed being with students like them for whom top grades came easily and church was a given but not a big deal like at First Baptist. There was a part of me that already liked that.

They asked me to join them to meet a couple who were coming down from the University of Illinois at Champagne-Urbana to see if they might start a chapter of the Wesley Foundation, a student-oriented organization that served near campuses all over the nation. I decided to go with them though I was suspicious of anybody coming from up north. I mean "everybody" knew that northerners were basically heretics, or so I thought in those days. We met in a building called Wesley Hall on campus that housed the Vanderbilt School of Religion. That was my first acquaintance with Ruth and Joe Brown Love. I listened for a while to what they had to say and then loudly said, "You're too liberal for me." Ruth and Joe Brown reminded me of that in later years when memory of it became a "cringe" moment. Suffice it to say that, along with friends on campus, I got involved with the start-up of the Wesley Foundation and never left it. That was the end of my involvement with the anti-intellectual Baptists of Nashville.[1]

Vim and I became friends on campus and in the Wesley Foundation and remained so for the next five years. We soon began to room together and there developed between us a friendship that lasted until his death a few years ago. We often double-dated and made sure that any friend either of us found became also a friend of the other. Under the tutelage of Ruth and Joe Brown Love we learned that Christianity was far more than the rank individualism of the evangelicals who teach that accepting Jesus as one's personal savior, no matter how one treated those who are different, was the essence of Christianity. We had believed the evangelicals that the "Holy Spirit" affected only individual Christians whereas historically the concept of the Holy Spirit was the early churches' way of moving on out from the confines of closed Scripture to address historically new problems. We learned for the first time the concept of social ethics that white evangelicals often condemn. We also learned that the reason they hate social ethics was that it would challenge the injustice of Apartheid and Jim Crowism that

1. The history of anti-intellectualism in America is well traced in Richard Hofstadter, *Anti-Intellectualism in American Life* (New York: Knopf, 1963).

evangelicals claimed Scripture supported. The Loves showed us that God was far bigger than we had been taught.

They introduced Vim and me to fellow students at Fisk University in a segregated part of Nashville. We often thereafter attended church at the Fisk Memorial Chapel on campus where we were privileged to hear sermons by the dean of the Chapel and pastor of the open church that met there on Sundays. His name was William Faulkner, and his title on campus was Dean. I had never heard such powerful sermons in my life. And to cap them off, the 100-voice Fisk University Choir would break into singing a spiritual just as Dean Faulkner would leave the pulpit to sit down after preaching. I sometimes sat there in the congregation and cried tears of spiritual happiness as the choir sang "Go Tell it On the Mountain" or a similar hymn. I was moved as I had never been moved in my life.

Once we asked Mama Howie, Vim's mother, to go with us. She reluctantly agreed but insisted that we sit on the last pew in the back of the sanctuary. I suppose she felt that sitting back there she would not be completely present. I'm sure it was hard on her. It must have gone against everything she had believed about segregation. We had not known it but it was a Sunday when they celebrated communion and Mama Howie refused to join us in partaking. That sad experience represented the wedge that was driven, mainly because of the Loves, between our Southern souls and our new open-minded hearts.

Faulkner invited members of the Wesley Foundation to his home. It was the first time we had ever been guests in a black family's home. Our very souls were being shaken to their core and it felt like we understood true freedom for the first time in our lives. We felt we now understood what the words of the Founding Fathers meant when they wrote the Declaration of Independence and the Constitution despite the fact that most of them had slaves; more than that we felt we now understood the teachings of Jesus as we never had before.

Our group graduated in June 1948. We all made Phi Beta Kappa and magna cum laude; our whole group was indebted to the Loves. In fact, I brought up the rear of the group in that I wasn't inducted into PBK until a few months after the others. Vim entered the Vanderbilt Medical School and I the Vanderbilt School of Religion the fall of the same year, 1948. Vim had quit his membership in Sigma Chi the year before; he was the only one of our group who had pledged as a freshman in the first place. He seemed relieved when he left the fraternity, as much as I eventually felt relief when I left the Baptists to welcome the Loves and help build the Wesley Foundation. We decided to share expenses and took a room near campus together. Vim kept a white Med-student jacket on a hook for me near his so that I could attend lectures at the Med school he knew I would want to hear. One I remember very well was by Prof. Dr. Smiley Blanton, professor of psychiatry. He was a Freudian and very humorous besides being very instructive. Once on a double date, Vim took the four of us to the anatomy lab at the Med School where the cadavres were lying that the Med students worked on. It was an evening when no one else was there. Vim at one point picked up a lung and tossed it to me just to shock our dates.

—chapter 4—

Belgium and North Africa

But before all that I had accepted an invitation from the Methodist Student Movement to accompany a "youth caravan" group assigned to visit Methodist mission stations in Belgium and North Africa for seven weeks in the summer of 1948. I was the translator for the group because the youth groups we met in both countries spoke French. I had majored in romance languages and philosophy and had been asked when I returned from the summer assignment to teach introductory French at Vanderbilt. Our youth caravan group crossed the Atlantic on one of the "liberty ships" that had transported troops during the War. We landed at Le Havre and went by train to Paris. We were assigned a B-class hotel for the night. Our group was scheduled to go then by train the next early afternoon to Brussels. I broke from the group that morning and went by myself to see the Jardins des Tuilleries and the Louvre. I got so involved in the beauty of them that I missed the train. I got to the Gare du Nord just in time to see the train pull out of the station. I had mixed emotions as I saw "my train" leave without me, but with my unused ticket I immediately arranged for a train the next day and looked forward to an evening in Paris by myself.

In Belgium we visited various mission stations where I learned of a different kind of bias. While at one of them I watched a Roman Catholic parade pass in front of the little Methodist church. But when the parade got exactly opposite the entrance to the mission station it stopped. The statue of a saint they were honoring was draped in black and lowered to pass in front of the station, after which the parade stopped and restored the statue to its perch and uncovered it to resume its path. Protestantism, that had been my whole life to that point, was anathema to Belgian Catholics. For the first time in my life I felt discriminated against! I was in the minority and

"hated." I had never thought of myself as being anything but in the majority
wherever I was and in the white privileged position of trying to bridge the
gap between whites and blacks. In the South, I reflected, we Protestants had
denigrated Catholics almost as much as we did blacks. Almost. Nonetheless
I was for the first time in my life in a scary, minority position. My eyes and
mind were being pried open in ways I had never imaged they would or
could be. Years later when asked to address a gathering of seminary presi-
dents at the Getty Institute in Los Angeles I mentioned that in the South
while bigotry against blacks was ingrained in the culture we were openly
taught to be biased against Catholics. With a chuckle I noted that we were
so much taught to be biased against Catholics that we didn't have time to be
biased against Jews!

But the Belgian experience shrank in perspective after we arrived in
Algiers. We were met at the dock there by a local Methodist pastor who took
us to Les Aiglons, a beautiful property in El Biar, way up the hill above the
city in a swank section of the suburbs of Algiers. I learned there what being
in a minority was really like. Algeria like Tunisia was a province of France,
in fact a *département*. Later in the1950s, the De Gaulle government would
grant them independence, but they were actually still at the time we were
there colonies under French rule.

Living for five weeks in a Muslim-dominate society was an experience that held me in good stead for later experiences in Palestine under
Jordanian rule and then Israeli. In North Africa I came to learn and honor
the history of Islam whereas in the Near East I came to learn and honor
the history of Palestinians, both Muslim and Christian. There were few
Christians indeed in North Africa. There were some who had converted
to Catholicism, certainly not many to Protestant missions, whereas in Palestine I became acquainted with Arab-speaking Christians some of whose
families' histories dated back to Crusader times and some even back to the
time of Christ. I had a great experience in North Africa. We spent time at a
Methodist mission station in Fort National in the Djura-Djura range of the
Atlas mountains. There we became acquainted with the Berbers, an ancient
people whose ancestry dates back to the Stone Age. Knowing that classical
Greeks called "barbarian" (coined from the tribal name Berber) any people
who were not Greek I guess I thought I'd encounter some primitive tribe.
On the contrary, they are a handsome people, taller than the average Algerian, and very intelligent. I made a friendship with a young Berber who was
studying medicine in France.

For two weeks I joined an Algerian French-speaking Boy Scout troop
who were camping up in the Atlas Mountains in an area called La Forêt
Bleue. I had never in my life, to that point, seen such natural beauty. We

slept a la belle étoile (in the open) on simple cots. The air was pure and the sounds echoing through the mountains were pristine. We would be awakened each morning by the flute of an Arab shepherd tending his flock somewhere nearby in those mountains. We couldn›t see him or his sheep, but it was amazingly beautiful to be awakened by such simple, pure music. It was an unforgettable experience.

Back at Vanderbilt that fall Vim and I found a room to share in a neighborhood close to campus. I started seminary at the School of Religion while he started at the Medical School (the fall of 1948). Despite heavy loads (I taught French to undergrads) we continued to be involved in the Wesley Foundation and became more and more aware of the evils of American racism. We were learning that racism wasn't limited to the South but that America is in essence a racist culture.[1] Still our immediate concerns were the intolerable situation in our own home culture. It was becoming more and more clear that the immense wealth accumulated by the plantations in ante-bellum South was amassed on the backs, the misery and the toil of blacks, and that the South in essence returned to a slave-based economy after the failure of Reconstruction and the beginnings of the Jim Crow laws that Congress increasingly condoned. These facts were not what we had been taught in school, not even at Vanderbilt where the "Agrarians" (a pro-Confederate group) like John Crowe Ransom, Donald Davidson and Walter Clyde Curry were highly honored.

The summer of 1949 became a turning-point for me personally. I spent the first six weeks at Massachusetts General Hospital in Boston taking a course in pastoral counseling. It was a good experience and deepened my concern about America's general racist culture that I found even in New England. The next six weeks were divided into two different programs. For three weeks I served as student-probation officer of the Juvenal Court System of the State of Connecticut, and for the last three weeks I joined the folk at the Christian Activities Council in Hartford with the bulk of the time spent as camp counselor at "House-in-the-Fields" in New Hartford out in the Connecticut countryside. There I met Miss Dora Geil Cargille who was also a counselor in the camp teaching the children classical ballet and modern dance movement. She had graduated from the New Jersey College for Women (NJC) that is now called Douglass College, part of Rutgers University.

Being wrapped up in doing our jobs as counselors Dora and I weren't much aware of each other until one particular evening. The kids in the

1. See Jim Grimsley, "Americans Are Nearly as Blind to Racism as Ever Before," *Los Angeles Times*, February 23, 2016.

camp were remanded there by the Juvenal Count System of Connecticut and a high percentage were just plain imps. I had seen her around the camp, for sure, but I thought that such a beautiful girl was beyond my reach and tended to ignore her and focussed instead on the kids. One evening, however, after we had bedded down the brats, we both happened to climb the same tree to escape them and have some respite. After assuring each other that we remembered the other's name we got better acquainted. After we got down out of the tree I guess I must have grimaced with pain. She asked if I could use a massage, that she had learned massage as a part of the dance program at NJC. Of course, I said, "Sure!" And that started a friendship that developed slowly over the next couple of years.

I don't recall seeing a black kid at the camp, but I do recall some of the racist comments the officers, with whom I was assigned to accompany to learn the probation system, made. It was a very full summer with the first six weeks studying patient counseling at Mass General in Boston, with the following three weeks as a student probation officer in Hartford and then three weeks as counselor in the camp. A couple of times other members of the Christian Activities Council teased me about having a Southern accent, and I learned from them that "one can take the boy out of the South but it's hard to take the South out of the boy." I had come so far in my thinking and in my own journey, with Vim, out of and away from Southern racism and culture that their teasing both hurt and helped me further along on the journey from bigotry to acknowledging the full humanity of those who are different. At the same time I was witnessing the forms racism took in those days in the Northeast, the cradle of the Abolitionist Movement in the nineteenth century, that was nonetheless almost as racist in some respects as the South.

My second year at the Vanderbilt School of Religion I was assistant to the editor of *Motive Magazine*, the publication nationally of the Methodist Student Movement. Vim was in his second year at Med School. We continued to room together and double-dated occasionally. We loved each other about as much as two guys can without having sex or interest in doing so. Both our schedules were tighter than ever, but we enjoyed our friendship and participating in events at the Wesley Foundation. We went to Fisk for Sunday services but not as often as we wanted. Dora and I corresponded a few times, but neither of us thought our friendship would develop into anything serious—yet. I took Greek and Hebrew and continued reading Latin as well as French texts. I really got into reading Hebrew and Prof. James Philip Hyatt kept challenging our grad school class with more and more difficult texts until one day he brought in the first publication of Dead Sea Scrolls from Qumran Cave 1 as soon as it was available. There were three of us in the class, the other two being doctoral students. I'll never forget the day he brought photos just published of the large Isaiah Scroll to class, set them in front of us, opened them to Isaiah Ch. 40, and said, "Read." Mind you these were photographs of the ancient scroll and he expected us to read the ancient script that we had never seen before. I got excited and was hooked for life.

I realized by that time that I was not interested in becoming a pastor but wanted to continue to read ancient texts and explore ancient cultures directly from texts, and through archaeology. I had not yet been introduced to field archaeology and though I visited many digs while affiliated with the American School of Oriental Research in East Jerusalem I never did participate in a working dig but I eagerly read reports I was interested in. We'll get to all that a bit later. When I mentioned my growing interest in biblical scholarship to Prof. Hyatt he told me about a new federal government program that sponsored study abroad introduced by Senator William Fulbright of Arkansas. I obtained the necessary paper work and submitted an application to do my last year of seminary in Paris.

Vim and I became more and more convinced that our country's original sin was not only slavery but following that the horrible racism that America continued to be cursed with. We were discovering that Jim Crow laws in the South, as terribly inhuman as they were, were often matched by racism in the rest of the country. It was simply more pronounced and obvious in the former slave states. My work off-campus as assistant to the editor of *Motive Magazine*, an organ of the Methodist Student Movement (MSM), that was produced in downtown Nashville, advanced my new perspective on human relations. The editor was Harold Ehrensperger, originally from Indiana. I had never before met anyone from Indiana as far as I knew. Harold was gay and that was really a new experience for me. After I made it clear that I was not interested we had a great relationship and I learned about the Methodist Church outside the American South. One issue we published included a picture of a black Jesus. It was at first a shock to my Southern soul to see the photo but once it was published I was very proud to be identified with the magazine.

— chapter 5 —

LAKE JUNALUSKA

As summer approached in 1950 Vim and I decided to apply for a position open at Lake Junaluska in western North Carolina as janitors of the Board of Education building at one end of the lake that was used each summer for the various groups that met there. The first group of that summer was made up of students associated with and involved in the MSM, so that Vim and I went there for the MSM annual meeting at the beginning of that summer before our work as janitors started. The General Board of Education of the United Methodist Church had hired us as janitors for the summer and they said we could begin our work during the MSM conference there. That way we already had digs on the second floor of the building we were to work (and sleep) in all summer. The MSM conference that took place at Junaluska each early June was by that time integrated. Black and white Methodist students were housed together and engaged in activities together, including swimming in the big pool not far from the Board of Education building.

But immediately after the students left Lake Junaluska reverted to total segregation. It was as though young Methodists could hear the Gospel message that their parents were deaf to. Since Vim and I were to remain for the whole summer we experienced a kind of cultural shock when the students left and the conferences for Methodist adults started. After we had arrived at Junaluska Vim and I applied for jobs in the big cafeteria in order to have our meals covered. So at that point we actually had two jobs for the summer, but the one in the cafeteria did not last long. Some of the black students who had participated in the two-week MSM conference in early June were also to work in the cafeteria. We had already met them and were delighted to have college friends we already knew to work with. When it came time for the help in the cafeteria to eat we got our food trays and joined the black students on the back porch where they were to eat. But that didn't sit well with the woman who had hired us. After the first couple of days Mrs. Christian, the dietitian, called us into her little office and laid down the law. We were to eat with the women out in the cafeteria itself. That meant we couldn't be with our friends for meals but would have to eat with old, white ladies out front. Vim and I knew exactly what that meant and told Mrs. Christian that we wanted to eat with our college friends. She said that was not permitted and that if we insisted on it we were fired. Right in front of her we took off our aprons, gave them to her, thanked her politely, and walked out. She stood there shocked, but we were not about to sponsor that kind of segregation at Lake Junaluska—or anywhere we worked for that matter. We had indeed been converted to true Christianity, and all because of Ruth and Joe Brown Love.

That left us with the job as janitors of the General Board of Education Building. We paid for meals in the cafeteria. We had not planned to spend that kind of money, but we managed. Vim and I enjoyed our one remaining job. Our duties were rather limited. We got up most mornings at about 5:30 and cleaned and prepared the various rooms in the building for whichever groups at the Lake each week would need the class rooms and other facilities through the rest of the summer. We were usually finished with the work by breakfast time, well before the groups started filing in for their seminars or study groups. The most we worked at that part of the job was two or three hours a morning. The one duty we had otherwise was at dusk to turn on the big klieg lights that lit up the big, white columns on the front porch of the building and then at about 10pm to turn them back off. The rest of the day we enjoyed the pool and got great tans. The pool was a cordoned-off section of the lake. We met some really nice girls whose families came with whatever group they were associated with. We had no problem getting dates for various events except that I was also a member of the double octet that was there for the summer to lead the singing each evening in the big pavilion where evening services took place, and couldn't meet my date until after services.

It didn't take long for us to realize, despite the fact that we had grown up in the South, that our black friends who also worked at the Lake had no place to swim. None. Vim and I decided that we would with a few of our black friends build a dock in a part of the Lake that white folks would not have to see. We bought some lumber and started to build a dock for them to swim off. But it wasn't long before our work was discovered and we were ordered to cease and desist, that we did not have permits to build such a dock. We knew that it was segregation pure and simple, but there was nothing we could do but stop. We certainly did not want to get our friends in trouble.

Older black folk knew that our plans were doomed from the start and kept their distance. We were defeated but undaunted.

I sang with the double octet most every evening that summer, but I learned from our black friends that the quartet that led the singing in the little church where the black help around the whole Lake worshipped and prayed lacked a second male voice, so I asked their pastor if I could join the group and make it a quartet. He agreed and I sang with the quartet whenever I didn't have to be in the double octet to lead singing in the big pavilion. A girl I dated during that time told me that her mother wanted to know what I was doing in "that Nigger church." I wasn't surprised at the question, so I told the girl friend to tell her mother that I was singing baritone, that's what I was doing. That was taken as sass by her sweet, "Christian," white mother and she forbad her daughter to date me any more. Again I was not surprised. Anyway, there were plenty of girls to date. That wasn't a problem. The problem was her mother's—and the whole of the USA's.

Our reputation became wide-spread among the regulars (white and black) at the Lake. White Methodists from around the country owned second homes and property on the hills around the lake and came to spend summers there. Even non-Methodists have found Lake Junaluska an attractive place to vacation, or to live. The televangelist, Billy Graham, lives with his wife in such a home at the Lake. Vim and I came to realize that segregation was also an economic issue. Ever since our minds were opened to the various ramifications of the struggle of America to live up to its origins and especially its Declaration of Independence and Constitution we came to see clearly the extent of the evils of Apartheid in the USA.

Evidently some folk at the Lake urged the head of the General Board of Education of the Methodist Church, Dr. John O. Gross, whose offices were in New York, to fire us from our job at the Board of Education building so that we would no longer be a threat to them. His office had hired us in the first place. He was coming to Junaluska on business anyway and after he had arrived asked us to meet with him. We, of course, responded that it would be our honor to meet with him. He said, "Let's meet on the porch of the building at such-and-such an hour." We thought that was considerate on his part since we not only worked at the building, we also had digs there in rooms up off a balcony. In other words, we sat with Dr. Gross, the head of the General Board of Education of the United Methodist Church, on the porch of our building, in three high-backed rocking chairs, in full view of everyone at the Lake who cared to look. I'm sure some who saw us were happy to see that Dr. Gross was going to fire us on the spot for being rabble-rousers. They couldn't call us "outside agitators," a favorite term white Southerners had for whites who came from up North to make trouble, so we were simply misguided rabble-rousers. But Gross did not fire us. On the contrary, he asked us a few questions about how the work was going and ended the conversation by thanking us for doing such a fine job. And that was it. The bigots had called out the big gun to shoot us down and, on the contrary, he warmly congratulated us on the work we were doing.

One day Vim and I were hitching a ride to get from one point on the Lake to another and a gentleman picked us up. He was very cordial at first. It was Mr. Love, the director of operations at the Lake. We introduced ourselves, or at least we started to, when he interrupted us and said, "Yeah, I know who you are. You seem like reasonable, well-meaning young men. You should stop all this non-sense and do something constructive—like work on the blood drive we're having right now at the Lake." Vim and I looked at each other and grinned. I responded by saying that we'd be delighted to work on the blood drive. We went right away to the office where the blood drive was being set up and offered our services. They said they needed us to stir up interest and also to organize cars to drive prospective donors into Ashville where the blood bank was. We immediately started talking up the drive around the Lake, including the black "help," and also organizing cars to transport donors. We integrated every car we recruited that drove donors into Ashville until it was suggested that they didn't need our help any further. We had made our mark despite the reign of bigotry at the Lake.

Mind you, this was 1950, five years before the Supreme Court's decision in Brown vs. Board of Education and six years before the Jim Crow "Southern Manifesto" drawn up by Southern Democrats in Congress.[1] The South was at the time almost totally made up of Democrats, the party that even in the North had opposed abolition and the Civil War. Earl Warren, a California Republican, was chief justice of the Supreme Court that in 1955 abolished segregated public schools. President Eisenhower proclaimed after the Brown vs. Board decision that appointing Warren was "the most damned-fool thing I've ever done." Even Eisenhower! And he was a Kansas Republican. The Republican Party was supposed to be the party of civil rights at the time. That was soon to change after Richard Nixon launched his "Southern strategy" in the 1968 presidential campaign. Vim and I understood the position of the Southerners in those days even while we fought it with all we had to fight it with; after all, we were both brought up to be "God-fearing Southern gentlemen"—meaning, of course, bigoted, except that one does not have to be Southern to be bigoted in the good old US of A as the enthusiastic followers of Donald Trump in 2016 have clearly shown.

---

1. Justin Driver, "60 Years Later, the Southern Manifesto Is as Alive as Ever," *Los Angeles Times*, March 1, 2016.

Our reputation around the lake apparently reached the highest levels of the Methodist hierarchy. Not long after the blood-drive effort we received an invitation from Bishop Paul Kern of eastern Tennessee, who was at the time vacationing in his summer home above the lake, to join him and friends for tea on a Sunday afternoon. Vim and I arrived at the Kern address high up a hill above the lake to find Bishop Kern had two other guests, Bishop Arthur J. Moore of Alabama, and Prof. Robert Martyr Hawkins, my professor of New Testament at the Vanderbilt School of Religion. I imagine that Bishop Kern thought that having Hawkins there would help his case. Actually Hawkins said nothing during the interview. Bishop Kern was the model of courtesy and asked us all to sit with him in his garden. Vim and I sat together on a two-seater bench while the bishops and Prof. Hawkins sat in individual garden chairs. It was a beautiful setting overlooking the lake. Bishop Moore, who was at the Lake to preach in the big pavilion that week, opened the conversation joined in by Bishop Kern. The force of the bishops' argument was that they appreciated what we were doing but that we had to go easy because we might "win the battle but lose the war." This was an argument we had heard before, and it frankly made us ill. Vim fell totally silent and it was up to me to engage the bishops. But even I was stunned by the position they took. After they had said what they had to say I finally spoke up. Mind you, we were the perfect Southern gentlemen in the presence of these prelates of the church and had sat cordially listening, but I sensed Vim beside me was silently about to explode. So I spoke up and said, "You'll have to forgive us, gentlemen. I guess we've taken your brotherhood sermons too seriously." With that Vim and I got up and the two of us walked calmly but deliberately out the garden gate. We didn't look back and therefore had no idea what their reaction was, and frankly at that point we didn't care.

That night Bishop Moore preached to a huge crowd in the big pavilion. I sat in the choir loft as a member of the double-octet while Vim sat with our dates for the evening out in the audience. All summer we had made sure that our behavior was that of Southern gentlemen, so we listened attentively to Bishop Moore's sermon as though nothing had happened in Bishop Kern's garden that afternoon. The bishop's sermon was a peroration against sin, there was nothing unusual about that, but when he made clear that sin was smoking and drinking I looked at Vim sitting in the audience with a pained expression. He looked disgusted. If all the good bishop could offer as sin was smoking and drinking we were vindicated in walking out the garden gate that afternoon. I knew Vim was thinking the same as me. What about racism and segregation? Didn't they deserve at least honorable mention?

We, of course, behaved ourselves through the rest of the service in the pavilion that evening and even with our dates after it. But after we had seen the young ladies to their respective lodgings with their families we let our genuine pain finally express itself. So, we figured, if smoking was a sin while Apartheid was obviously not, maybe, we thought, we should try smoking. We forthwith went to the tuck shop near the swimming area and bought a package of Chesterfields and some matches. Frankly after nothing but rejection the whole summer long in our efforts to do what we understood was the Christian thing to do at a totally segregated Church conference facility we finally just let our hurt hang out for all to see. We had no idea what to do with the package of cigarettes so Vim just put it in a pocket, but later when we saw Bishop Moore walking toward us on the same path Vim got a cigarette out and lit it up practically in his face as he passed us. Being brought up to be Southern gentlemen we were not openly rude, mind you, but we knew he'd recognize us as he passed and we were not about to let the opportunity pass. He looked at us smiling but said nothing, nor we.

We continued working our job the remainder of the summer, enjoying the swimming and the young ladies as they came and left with their families. In July Vim in fact met a young lady he was to marry that fall. We "behaved" ourselves as well as we could and wanted to honor Dr. Gross' trust in us and didn't mount any further campaigns to integrate Lake Junaluska. We did, however, continue to "fraternize" with the blacks we knew at the Lake. We figured that even the highest authorities of the Church could not stop us from seeing our friends. In early August I received a letter forwarded from home affirming the Fulbright Grant I'd applied for with details on how to proceed. I had already received a preliminary acceptance but this was the letter that gave me detailed instructions on where to be and how and when to board ship for France. I was overjoyed, but I saw that Vim was rather quiet about it. When I saw him later that day coming up from swimming he didn't even crack a smile. We had been bosom buddies for over five years and he had always seemed happy to see me, even across campus, but this meant we'd be apart for a full year—at least. I understood but had hoped he'd celebrate with me.

— chapter 6 —

A WEDDING IN PARIS

In addition I also heard about the same time from Dora Cargille, the young lady I'd met in Connecticut the previous summer. I was delighted and began to make plans to go see her before I boarded the ship. Back home while I was packing a trunk to send ahead, my mother, who had never left home except in the company of another adult, expressed bafflement that I was preparing to leave for a foreign company with ease and no anxiety. She didn't understand how I could do all that. I had already been away from home for several years, including the summer in Europe and North Africa, but my blessed mother said she didn't understand how I could keep in mind all I had to do. She also knew I planned to go see Dora before I sailed. I still admire her to this day for not making me feel guilty for not staying home to take care of her and my father. My sister, Nell, secretly kept after me to follow my own stars and not stay home, as the last of eight children, to take care of my aging parents. In due course I got all my gear checked to accompany me on the train to go to New York.

When I checked in to the hotel in the big city where the Fulbrighters were gathering I was shocked to see that the hotel staff, room cleaners and others, were white. As a Southerner I had never imagined that white women would accept such menial jobs. They were probably recent immigrants from Europe. Recent immigrants have always had a hard time in the first decades after arriving no matter where they came from—Germany, Scotland, Ireland, Italy, Poland, etc. I recalled seeing a sign that read "Irish need not apply." Each generation usually shuns recent immigrants. We are a nation of immigrants each after rising up the cultural and political ladder feeling the need somehow to shut the door of immigration. Racism and xenophobia continue as national traits despite the intentions of the "founders" of the country expressed in the poem by Emma Lazarus on the Statue of Liberty. Maybe the disconnect between what the founders thought and wrote and the fact that they pretty much all had slaves set the conflicted tone for the future of the country.

I did indeed go up to Hartford to see Dora after I'd checked in at the hotel in New York. Vim and I had had our hair cut military style for the summer's work (and for swimming) at Junaluska and that was the first thing Dora noticed when she met my bus in Hartford. She later told me that the last thing she wanted was to marry a boy with a crew cut. We had a good visit anyway. She was still staying at the Christian Activities Council on Farmington Avenue which was located near the Hartford Seminary Foundation campus. We spent a good bit of the day before I had to return to New York walking the campus and getting better acquainted. She asked me if I had to go back to New York by bus because otherwise she'd like us to ride her motorcycle down to her home in Newark NJ to meet her parents before I boarded ship. I said I'd like to meet them. I wasn't so keen about meeting her family, but I wanted to be with her as long as possible in any case. I later learned that Vim proposed to a young lady who had been at Junaluska for a leadership conference in July, whom he married that fall.

My ship was to leave at noon the next day so we arrived on Dora's bike at her home in Arlington NJ about 5 am. She woke her parents so we could meet. Her mother, Esther Cargille, seemed to be glad to meet me, even happy, while her father, Ralph P. Cargille, did not seem so pleased. In fact he told her in my presence that he wasn't at all sure about me. He had earlier told her that if she married a Southerner she would be like a fish out of water. He clearly did not yet know me well. Soon after we arrived Esther called Dora's older brother, Jim, and his wife, Chloe, asking them to gather for breakfast as soon as they could get there. Dora and I went by bus to New York later that morning. While waiting for my ship to load passengers Dora and I stopped in a restaurant on the lower floor of Penn Station for a coffee. We agreed to have a date upon my return to the States the following summer and as a token of the agreement I gave her my Phi Beta Kappa key. I never wore it and couldn't imagine I'd need it in Europe and at the same time couldn't afford a "date ring" so I asked her to let the PBK key be a token of our mutual promise to have a date upon my return. Correspondence during the year re-signified the agreement from a promise for a date to something more lasting.

The year in Paris studying at the Ecole Libre de Théologie Protestante and at the Ecole des Hautes Etudes of the University of Paris was another broadening experience. The French seemed to accept blacks from the colonies or from the USA as equals, and that was an eye-opener. Blacks were definitely in a distinct minority so the experience was somewhat limited. Late that fall I went hiking with an American friend I had met at the Clube Américain on Boulevard Aragot along the Loire river exploring a few of the magnificent chateaux that line the river. At Christmas I flew back down to Algeria to spend the holiday with friends I'd made there two years earlier. After I arrived in Algiers I sent Dora a telegram: "Christmas Eve until you come." In further correspondence we laid plans for her to come over at the end of the year.

She did indeed come over with her motorcycle. I met her in early May at Le Havre and saw the green motorcycle hoisted out of the hold of the ship onto the pier. Together we rode the bike to Paris in the rain but stayed for the night at a little auberge in St. Aubin about half-way there. Mme Dauchez, my logeuse, had another bedroom for Dora to occupy during the six weeks left in my school year. She rode the bike around Paris exploring areas even I had not seen since I was engrossed in my studies. I had requested exams in all the courses I had taken so that a transcript could be transmitted back to Vanderbilt. This was at the insistence of Prof. Hyatt who then saw to it that I receive the B.D. degree from Vanderbilt in absentia. We were married on June 30th, 1951, first at the Mairie of the Sixth Arrondissement in the morning and then at the little Temple Protestant on Rue Madame nearby that afternoon. I had started already in January—just in case—preparing the paper work necessary for an American couple to get married in France. This entailed numerous trips to the American Embassy and managing other red tape, but it worked. We were given a *Carnet de Famille* as evidence of the nuptials and that is all we have to prove we were married. For our *lune de miel* we rode around Europe on the bike for about six weeks. Everywhere we went people would call the bike *le monstre vert*. While to us it was a small motorcycle by American standards there it appeared quite large. We sailed on the same ship, the De Grasse, to return to the States. We arrived back at her home in Jersey for a couple of weeks before heading to Cincinnati on the bike.

— chapter 7 —

HEBREW UNION COLLEGE

I intended to go on to graduate school at Yale in New Testament after a
year studying Jewish backgrounds at the Hebrew Union College (HUC) in
Cincinnati. That was the intention. In Cincinnati we found a little apartment in Avondale, a Jewish neighborhood at the time, where we lived for
a year. After that year I was so fascinated with all that I was learning about
Bible and Early or Second Temple Judaism that I decided to stay on and
maybe pick up the idea of going to Yale later on for a doctorate in New
Testament. Living and studying with Jews for the three full years we were
in Cincinnati further opened my mind and also many doors that I had not
known even existed. I was by now four years out of the South and what I had
learned about God's immense world outside born-again Christianity was
both exciting and challenging.

The first year we were in Cincinnati Dora worked downtown in a department store, but beginning with the second year she was a member of the
faculty at the University of Cincinnati teaching modern dance and music
for dance. Dora's apparently innate ability to improvise at both the piano
and the organ stood her again in good stead. On Sundays she was organist
at a Methodist Church in St. Thomas, Kentucky, across the Ohio River. The
summers of 1953 and '54 we drove out to Colorado College in Colorado
Springs so Dora could study with Hanya Holm, a prominent figure in the
world of dance in New York who taught summers at Colorado College. That
first summer I started writing the dissertation required for getting a doctorate and the second summer I oversaw its being typed (there were no com-
puters in those days). I had majored, so to speak, in Bible (the Hebrew Bible)
and in Hellenistic pre-Christian Judaism at HUC—very good preparation
for one interested in work in New Testament. The dissertation was titled

"Suffering as Divine Disicipline in the Old Testament and Post-biblical Judaism." It was a clumsy title, but then most dissertations have awkward titles. It was the beginning of my life-long interest and study of the uses of adversity in the hands of the One God of All, as professed in the Tanak or Hebrew Old Testament.

My father, bless his heart, had funded our buying a car after we'd had only the motorcycle through the rather harsh first winter we were in Cincinnati to get around the city—Dora to her work and I to the HUC campus. He asked that I send Muddy (my mom) $50 a month to reimburse him what he'd paid for the car. A year or so later after I'd faithfully for a year sent Mom the monthly checks, Daddy said, "From now continue to set aside for yourselves the fifty a month in order to buy the next car when you need it." I did that and have monthly saved the money necessary ever since so that we've never bought a car on credit but with cash. He reminded me of what he'd often told me, that "cheap is expensive." I also found that buying on credit means one pays much more for a car over what paying cash means. When I was about twelve years old I had accumulated enough dimes and quarters from mowing lawns to buy a much-needed pair of new jeans. But I knew, even though I'd made the money myself, I'd have to ask my father if I could buy a new pair. I told him I'd seen a pair I liked at Mr. Osier's Dry-Goods Store up on McLemore Avenue. He asked me how much money I had. I told him and he said, "Wait, son, until you can put another dollar with what you have and buy the best Mr. Osier has." I have in later years learned that not only is cheap expensive but that is the reason the working poor so often stay in poverty and can't extricate themselves. They can only afford to buy what they need cheap, and it doesn't last long before they have the expense of repairing it or buying something new, again cheap—a kind of vicious circle.

When I'd finished defending the dissertation, with I believe all the faculty at HUC present (an honor in itself), I left the building to join Dora, who had been waiting in our car, packed to the gills, and we headed for Rochester NY. Back before we had left for Colorado Springs that May I had gotten a call from the president of Colgate Rochester Divinity School (CRDS) asking me up to visit with him and some of the faculty about a position that had just come open there to teach Old Testament. The professor, Bernhard Word Anderson, had just informed the president that he had accepted a post as dean of the Drew University Divinity School in Madison NJ. The president made it clear that I was being asked to come up for a year only until they could secure a prominent successor for Anderson. I wasn't too interested because I wanted to go on to Yale to get a second doctorate in New Testament. They made our visit to see the campus very attractive and we finally agreed to accept the offer as long as it was for the one year only. That was what they wanted as well.

The graduation ceremonies for the Hebrew Union College each year were held at the Plum Street Temple in Cincinnati. My best friend during the time we were at HUC was Jakob Josef Petuchowski (*'alov ha-shalom*), who had managed to escape Europe to London before the war and who later became professor of rabbinics at HUC. As doctoral graduands we were assigned places together in the processional just behind the rabbinic students who were there to receive *semichah*, or ordination. This was in June 1955. I was just ahead of Jake in the procession, so that when I went to mount the stairs up the *bimah* President Nelson Glueck was looking at his notes or program or whatever, and he did not see that I was the next in line. As I approached him he started to raise his hands to place them on my shoulders as he had done for the rabbinic ordinands just ahead of me. This *goy* almost got *semichah*! Alas, he caught himself just in time and lowered them to shake my hand, and congratulate me, instead of putting them on my shoulders.

During the full three years I was a grad student at HUC I continued to be affiliated with the Methodist Church, but as I was finishing up and preparing for the dissertation defense I heard from an official in the Memphis Conference of the Methodist Church that the bishop of the Conference had decided that I "was not eligible for the Methodist ministry." I was shocked. I knew that ¶248 of the Methodist Book of Disicipline stipulated that a candidate for "full connection" (ordination) in a Conference had to be under the direct supervision of the District Superintendent of the area where the candidate studied. The chair of the Conference committee had interpreted the regulation in my case as fulfilled by keeping in close touch with the local Superintendent. In my case I had fellowships for doctoral study that forbade me to do any kind of work while a fellow studying for a degree. The bishop, William T. Watkins of the Memphis Conference, however, did not support the Superintendent's interpretation of the paragraph in question and summarily dismissed all I had done to reach full ordination. I was stunned but undaunted. My father had been an Elder in the Cumberland Presbyterian Church in Memphis which led me to inquire of two local Presbyterian pastors near HUC what I would need to do to seek ordination in the local Presbytery. Both, it turned out, had been former Methodists themselves and warmly welcomed me into the process of being ordained in the Presbytery of Cincinnati. Dora and I continued to be Presbyterian for the next forty years. Thereafter we found a wonderful Episcopal Parish near our home in Claremont where we have communed ever since.

There were no blacks or even women at HUC back in those days, and accepting women in the rabbinate was still some time off. As I look back on my experience at HUC I reflect on how totally anti-Zionist HUC was. Not a single member of the faculty at the time was Zionist. Classical Reform Judaism, like Orthodox Jewry but for quite different reasons, was generally non-Zionist. The whole community was still in trauma over the just-concluded Nazi holocaust. No Jewish organization had done more in the 1930s and 40s to rescue Jews from Hitler's diabolic "final solution" than Reform Judaism. Everyone there was conscious of the so-called Reform "mission of Israel." American Reform Judaism was born of the Jüdische Wissenschaft movement in mid-nineteenth century Germany. The famous rabbis, Isaac Meyer Wise and Stephen Wise, immigrants from Germany, founded American Reform Judaism soon after they immigrated. They wrote and spoke often of their belief that America was God's true Zion. The mission of the Reform movement was for Jews to exit their ghettoes and live lives of Torah out in the "real" world. They were not at all interested in the founding of a nation-ghetto even if it was called Israel. In their minds it would simply be the largest ghetto Jews had ever known. HUC was the first Jewish institution of higher education to instigate a doctoral program for non-Jews. They apparently had little trouble raising the money among Reform Jews necessary for the program. I was the second non-Jew to receive the PhD from HUC.

My years at HUC started only three years after the United Nations voted to partition Palestine. Even the ortho-practicing Jews at the College were anti-Zionist, but it should be remembered that Orthodox Judaism at that time was also anti-Zionist except that the Orthodox view was that Israel could be re-established (after nearly 2000 years) only when Messiah came, or by God in God's good time. One ortho-practicing faculty member at the time joked that the Jewish state over there should be called Judea, or Judah, not Israel.

Conservative Judaism was founded by Solomon Schechter in 1901 in large part over against Reform Judaism to support the Zionist cause. Schechter also founded the Jewish Theological Seminary in New York City. Most Jews, Reform and Orthodox, here in the second decade of the 21st century are now Zionist. The big shift took place during and just after the Six-Day War in June 1967 except that current Zionism is now also religious whereas the original Zionists inspired by Theodor Hertzl at the end of the nineteenth century were almost totally secular and certainly non-religious. It was a cultural experiment in origin. In fact, the kibbutzim founded by early Zionist groups were for the most part non-observant, and very conscious of being good neighbors with the Palestinians. The Six-Day War of 1967 changed the whole scene largely because they viewed the victory of the Six-Day War a *neis*, a miracle, and hence the start of a "messianic era." Now nearly all Jews support the State of Israel, and many young Jews do not know the history of Zionism. They essentially demonize all Palestinians because a few throw rocks or lob grenades at the Israeli wall erected by Israel to protect Jews. Those who launch rockets from Gaza belong to Hamas, the enemy of most Palestinians. Baffled Palestinians ask the question, "What is ethical about Western nations joining to make Palestinians give up or sell their homes to solve our Christian anti-Semitism?"

As will be suggested later in this essay, the Arab-Palestinian conflict will be resolved only when the original Zionist policies and philosophy are revived and Israel becomes the Palestinians' best friend. God knows, no Arab state in the region truly supports the Palestinians, even Jordan. They use it to advance their own views of the *Ummah Arabiyah*, not to help the Palestinian people. If current Zionists would re-affirm classical Reform Judaism's understanding of the "Mission of Israel" the problem could be solved in their and the Palestinians' favor. The view of the writer is that the old expression and belief advanced by Jesus speaking to the woman at the well in Sychar, that "salvation comes from the Jews" (John 4:22), will be realized when Judaism overtakes Zionism to reverse what has happened since the Six-Day War. I am biased about Jews and Judaism and usually vote for whatever Jew is on a ballot I have the privilege to mark. Long before it showed up on FaceBook with tongue in cheek, I answered an evangelical Christian's question asking how I could vote for a socialist Jew (meaning Bernie Sanders) with the response, "Well, we worship one on Sundays." If I had wanted to counter his remark on its own level I might well have asked back, "How can a true Christian support an immoral bigot like Donald Trump?"

— chapter 8 —

COLGATE ROCHESTER DIVINITY SCHOOL

The president at CRDS, Wilbour Eddy Saunders, presented himself as a father figure for the young (26 years old) couple when he insisted that we sell the recreational vehicle (RV) we had owned in Cincinnati for two years as our home and come live in a building on campus. Dora felt we were sacrificing a great deal to comply, but she agreed to sell it. We realized some profit from selling it and were able to supplement the institutional furnishings in the Axling House apartment where we were to live.

It was kind of fun adapting to faculty status the first years at CRDS. Many students assumed I was another student like them, that is, until I met my first class! Maybe I was having too much fun being taken for a student, but they soon learned who I was. But how was I to teach the introduction of Old Testament course when I'd never done so? I solved that problem by translating chapter by chapter a new book that had just been published before I left France, Adolphe Lods' *Histoire de la Littérature Hébraic et Juive depuis les Origines jusqu'a l'an 135*. I remember having carefully to cut the pages open as I read it. (Books in Europe in those days, in contrast to those produced in America, were always published paper-back in folios with the pages uncut.) There was one black student in the class, but he was very light complexioned and by his own admission often "passed." I was to run into bigotry in Rochester on a large scale later on.

I remember enjoying learning to teach those first months at CRDS. As the autumn months filed past I learned what winter could be like. Dora loved skiing so snow to her was a delight. President Saunders liked to point out that Rochester had two seasons, winter and July 4th. That, of course, is not really true, but it seemed to fit that first year quite well as we adapted to upstate climate. Things moved rather rapidly for Dora and me both. Dora

44

got a job in a department store that year. I began to notice by December that I had rather frequent visits from members of the faculty who would come to my office and engage in seemingly idle conversation. I had begun to get involved in the Society of Biblical Literature (SBL), the guild for professors of Bible in the country (and increasingly the guild for professors all over the world), and even offered a paper in one of the sections in December of that year. The SBL, and its sister guilds, met three years out of four after Christmas at Union Theological Seminary in New York City (where it had been founded in 1875). That was great for us because we had planned to go down to be with Dora's family in north Jersey for the holidays. It is a simple bus trip from near their home to the Port Authority Building in New York where all Jersey bus lines to the city terminate. She persuaded me to join in some classes that she took, especially those under Hanya Holm. Holm choreographed the Broadway musical "Kiss me, Kate."

As we drove back from Jersey to Rochester I had to stop several times to let Dora out to heave-ho. We both thought she had caught the flu or something like it. We soon found that was not the case. We learned in early January that she was pregnant. In the meantime the casual visits from faculty members increased until I was invited to accept a position as Assistant Professor for three years. This time instead of rejecting the offer, as I otherwise would have done, I let it be known that we were interested—along with the news that we were going to be a family. Almost as soon as I accepted the offer, President Saunders, who had sort of sponsored us from the beginning of our arrival, suggested that I let CRDS have the manuscript of my dissertation to publish as a special edition of its annual seminary bulletin. I happily agreed and *Suffering as Divine Discipline* was published that spring. Saunders also procured the mailing list of the SBL and had the issue mailed to each member.[1]

After our son, Robin David, was born (2 September 1955) Dora was invited to be instructor in modern dance in the Physical Education Department of the University of Rochester. She accepted and remained a member of that faculty until she had to relinquish it to come live with me in Jerusalem in 1962. But that is getting ahead of ourselves.

After we had lived in Axling House on campus Dr. Saunders suggested that we consider buying the home of a colleague who was leaving CRDS to join another faculty elsewhere. The home was only a half-block away on Highland Parkway and beautifully located. But they were asking $16,000 (mind you, this was 1956 dollars) and Dora and I had no idea where to find

1. Sanders, ed., "Suffering as Divine Discipline in the Old Testament and Post-Biblical Judaism." Special issue. *Colgate Rochester Divinity School Bulletin* 28 (1955).

that kind of money. Dr. Saunders stood again in the batter's box and said that CRDS would be happy to hold the mortgage at 4% per annum with no down payment. We immediately accepted but then it became a question of how to furnish our beautiful new home. Again Dr. Saunders stepped up and invited us to accompany him to go through the furniture stored in the garrett of his wife's family's mansion on Prince Street—a top address in those days in Rochester. Every piece of furniture we expressed interest in was delivered to our new home on Highland Parkway. Sixty years later we still have a few pieces of that precious furniture in our home in Claremont CA. I have sometimes wondered if a piece or two should not be taken to an episode of *Antiques Road Show!*

How was I to repay such generosity? By loyalty to CRDS as long as Dr. Saunders was president, for sure. But it also inspired me to write up some follow-up work to the dissertation and submit it for publication. I continued to offer papers at the SBL but I also wrote a book that Harper Brothers Publishers accepted and published early in 1961 as *The Old Testament in the Cross*. I also had continued to work on the Dead Sea Scrolls as they were published and available for study. Out of that work I wrote a paper I titled "Habakkuk at Qumran, Paul and the Old Testament," in which I noted the different interpretations of Habakkuk 2:4 in the Habakkuk Commentary Scroll from Qumran Cave 1, in Paul's Epistles, in the Epistle to the Hebrews and compare them with what current critical scholarship understood the passage in Habakkuk itself to mean. It is a crucial verse in Paul's theology, as is well known, but it was the different meanings given the passage at Qumran and in the early Greek translations of Habakkuk that interested me most—in comparison with what scholarship at the time said was its "original" meaning in Habakkuk.[2]

Apparently on the basis of the dissertation and of the book published by Harpers I received an invitation from the University of Chicago to read a paper to the faculty there of the University of Chicago Divinity School. I accepted and also sent them the paper on Habakkuk to consider for publication. They published it in the *Journal of Religion*, one of the prominent journals in our field. The paper I read for the faculty was one I had developed on the original meanings of Genesis chapter one (Genesis 1–2:4a). The paper was well received, and I was soon offered a position at the University of Chicago Divinity School.[3]

2. Sanders, "Habakkuk in Qumran, Paul and the Old Testament," *Journal of Religion* 39 (1959) 232–44.

3. Sanders, "God Is God," *Year-Book 1972/73*, Ecumenical Institute (Jerusalem, 1974) 103–27.

In the meantime other developments were afoot. With Dr. Saunders' intervention I was able the summer of 1959 to go on a traveling seminar to Israel sponsored by New York University. The cost was beyond our means as a family though Dora morally supported my going. Dr. Saunders spoke by phone with an old friend, Murray Newman, the rabbi of Rodeph Shalom Synagogue in New York City, and before I could express appreciation for his efforts I received the necessary funds in the mail. On my way coming back through New York I called on Rabbi Newman in his offices on Central Park West and expressed thanks personally.

— chapter 9 —

THE PSALMS SCROLL

The traveling seminar lasted six weeks. It was very informative and I thoroughly enjoyed visiting several archaeological sites. As a group we got rather weary of the constant pro-Zionist slant of the speeches, but otherwise it was a success. My impression on the whole was that Israel was basically at that point (1959) a refuge for European Jews who had fled European anti-semitism, not just Naziism, and for Jews from Arab countries after Israel declared its independence and statehood. Later the population would become more diverse. At the conclusion of the seminar I crossed through the Mandelbaum Gate on the Nablus Road into the Old City and the West Bank. I immediately went to the American School of Oriental Research (ASOR, now titled The Albright Institute) on Salah ed-Dhin Street north out of Herod's Gate. There I was met by Wadiah, one of the staff of the School, who showed me to my room. I had ties with the ASOR in America and had written ahead that I would be arriving. Crossing through the Gate was an amazing experience of passing from one civilization to a totally different one. Whereas Israel felt like an extension of Europe the Old City felt far more like what I had known a decade earlier in North Africa. North Africa was at the time a group of French colonies and Palestine a former British mandate territory. Otherwise they were both very Near Eastern and very different from Israel. I engaged in some of the activities of the American School, especially field trips, but had only a week before I would have to return to duties in Rochester.

The most significant event I experienced at the Jerusalem School occurred at dinner one night where Prof. Frank Cross, who had just the year before left McCormick Seminary in Chicago to join the Harvard Divinity School faculty as successor of Prof. Robert Pfeiffer, was present. There were some francophone guests there with whom I was happy to speak French, not thinking how this might leave anyone out of the conversation. But Cross spoke up and apologized that he was "monolingual." I knew he meant speaking English because he was a renowned scholar of ancient Near Eastern languages and fluent in reading French and German. Being a little embarrassed I spoke only English at the table thereafter. After dinner, however, as was the custom at the School, a number of us gathered in the garden to chat with Prof. Marvin Pope of Yale. But before I could join the group Prof. Cross, who was retreating to his room to work on his Cave 4 lot of Qumran fragments, stopped me to ask if I'd like to accompany him the next morning to see the Scrollery at the Palestine Archaeological Museum (PAM, later the Rockefeller Museum/Israel Museum Number Two). I immediately responded that it would be an honor.

At the museum Cross introduced me to those of the Cave 4 Team who were already at work, notably Monsignor Patrick Skehan and Abbé Josef Milik. We then went to Cross' table which was piled with biblical fragments from Cave 4, those Cross was assigned to study and publish. I was just thrilled to be in such company when all of a sudden Cross picked up a fragment and asked if I could identify it. It was from Jeremiah chapter 8. I looked at it and read it off filling in the lacunae with words I knew from the passage in the Masoretic Text. Cross was apparently impressed. I was not. The script was beautifully preserved on that fragment and I felt that if I could not read it I should return my doctoral degree to the Hebrew Union College. In fact, it took me back to the moment over a decade earlier when Prof. Hyatt put the newly published photos of the Isaiah Scroll from Cave 1 in front of us and said, "Read." I stayed with Cross, at his invitation, until it was time to return to the American School for lunch. Nothing more was said about it. In fact, I spent the little time I had left going on field trips with fellows at the American School to sites on the West Bank. One mandatory trip in the Jerusalem area was to walk through (the so-called) Hezekiah's Tunnel. Cross warned us that we might run into Arab women from nearby Abu Diis and other villages doing their weekly wash, and we did indeed. The most memorable field trip was to the Qumran dig and nearby caves. As our command car approached the area all one could see from the access road (nothing but parallel tracks in the desert winding up to the ruins of the Qumran community's buildings) was a huge camel with a big black crow sitting on its back doing its job of picking nits from the camel's furry skin. If one goes to that area today one does so on a well-paved road leading to a tourist welcome shop with ample modern amenities.

Not long after I had returned to Rochester and resumed teaching that fall I got a phone call at our home from Prof. Cross. He came directly to the point asking if I would be open to going out to Jerusalem to work on a large scroll as yet unopened. I to this day do not know how I responded. I was almost speechless. But, of course, I said I'd be happy to do so. I added that I had a sabbatical coming up at CRDS for the year 1961–62 and didn't know if I could manage to do it earlier, but Cross assured me that that would work out splendidly. He explained that the administration of the ASOR was still working on funding. He did not elaborate, and it wasn't necessary. I immediately spoke with Dr. Saunders about the phone call and he was obviously pleased for me. In due course I was awarded a Guggenheim Fellowship and Cross saw to it that I was appointed Annual Professor at the ASOR in East Jerusalem for the year 1961–62 affording me ample room and board for the year. All the various pieces of the puzzle were falling into place very nicely.

I learned from Henry Detweiler of Cornell University (just down the road from Rochester), the president of the corporation of the ASOR at the time, that negotiations were still going on to secure the money necessary to release the scroll I was to work on. Mr. and Mrs. Kenneth Bechtel of San Francisco were interested in funding the release but they of course wanted it to be tax-exempt, which meant that they wished to donate the money to the ASOR. The USA government, however, would have prohibited their using the ASOR as a "conduit" of funds just so they would be tax-exempt—sort of like laundering monies, I suppose. They somehow eventually worked it out, but the government of the Hashemite Kingdom of Jordan had to agree to the arrangement since it had responsibility for the administrative government of the West Bank and East Jerusalem, including the Palestine Archaeological Museum where the scrolls were stored and studied.

Dean Gerald Brower at the University of Chicago Divinity School, knowing nothing of any of the above, kept the pressure on for an answer to their invitation to join the faculty there. Since at the moment there were still some factors as yet unknown, such as the funding for the Scroll and the Guggenheim, all I could say to Brower was that I had plans to be in Jerusalem in 1961–62 and could not accept their invitation until after that. He was insistent that I had to accept right away or the offer was off. I said that I regretted that I could not accept the invitation. I was not about to return to Cross and tell him I couldn't accept the appointment to unroll the scroll. In fact, I had no hesitation about the decision; I was simply baffled by Dean Brower's intransigence.

Plans to go out to Jerusalem took shape in due course and I sailed on the passenger liner, the United States, the second week of September 1961. We rented our home in Rochester for the year and Dora went to live in New Jersey with our son, Robin David, at her brother's home in Little Falls. She planned to commute into New York to work in modern dance for the year.

I wished they could be with me but I wanted to support her career just as she'd always supported mine. Though I did not know it when I booked passage on the ship the SS United States was to be on a cruise for that voyage. It called at Funchal Madeira, a Portugese colony in the Atlantic off the coast of Morocco, at Gibralta, a British port, and then at Majorca in the Mediterranean. In all it took about ten days to reach Naples where I transferred to the SS Excalibur, an all-first-class ship, for the voyage to Beirut after a stop at Alexandria for ship maintenance. I took my copy of the Hebrew Bible (BHK in those days) with me and spent the extra time on the voyage memorizing the 150 Hebrew Psalms. Cross had told me that a couple of fragments pried loose from the outside of the Scroll were from the Book of Psalms. When I got to Beirut I called on Abbés Starkey and Milik who were in residence at the French School of Archaeology there. I had visited with Cross and other members of the Cave 4 Team back in the States before sailing asking all of them what they knew about unrolling an ancient scroll. Much to my regret there was precious little at that point published or unpublished on the topic. (All those I visited were working with fragments of various sizes but none with a full scroll, and there was no technical report yet at that point on the unrolling of the Cave 1 scrolls.) I stayed with friends from the ship who were on the faculty at the American University of Beirut (AUB). After I had secured my trunk and other baggage from the ship I reserved space on a service taxi from Beirut to Amman thence to Jerusalem. That was the way folk traveled in those days. The service taxi is a scheduled taxi which whenever filled up left for its destination. They were almost invariably Mercedes Benz cars. The driver with no garages along the way had to be a mechanic as well as driver and needed an auto that could manage long trips in the desert.

When I was settled in my room at the American School I met with the director, Paul W. Lapp, and he explained that since I would not have my family with me until the next spring he would use the Annual Professor's Apartment at the School for visiting scholars until Dora arrived. That was fine with me. Lapp was as acting director of the American School also a member of the board of trustees of the Palestine Archaeological Museum (PAM). He explained that since the permission for me to start work on the scroll had not yet arrived from the Department of Antiquities in Amman I should engage myself in school activities, especially field trips, of the ASOR. I agreed and joined him and the two fellows appointed to the School that year on trips to Qumran and other digs in Palestine and then a long trip north with Lapp along the coast of Syria (after getting there by way of Amman) into Turkey and back. The trip lasted a good ten days and was very instructive. I learned a lot from Lapp and was grateful for the experience. Using the same ASOR command car I led a school trip across the Jordan to the ancient ruins south of Amman at Petra—one of the most stunning sites anywhere in the area. The permission from Amman arrived a few days after we arrived back from the trip. I was eager and ready to start though privately apprehensive about whether I would be up to the task.

I had met Père Roland de Vaux, director of the Ecole biblique et archéologique on Nablus Road in Jerusalem (also in East Jerusalem). De Vaux was also chair of the board of the PAM. De Vaux, Lapp, Yusef Sa'ad, and I met in the little individual lab room I was assigned for the task of unrolling the scroll. Yusef Sa'ad was a Palestinian Christian who served as Secretary of the Museum. After the three gentlemen had introduced me to my work space Sa'ad went to the vault of the museum, got the scroll, brought it into my lab room and placed it on a table covered with long, brown paper strips. De Vaux handed me the box that held the scroll and then the three backed out of the room and shut the door clearly indicating that it was my job to unroll and study the scroll—or it would unroll me! There I was alone with the two-millenia-old scroll, ugly yet beautiful as one could imagine, staring me in the face. The first thing I did was fall to my knees and pray. The room had three large windows that looked out east to both the Mount of Olives and Mount Scopus. Under the windows was a long built-in table that the staff of the museum had covered with clean, brown wrapping paper. I placed the scroll on the table and gently coaxed the outside fragments off. These were, I assumed, the ones Cross said they had been able to peek under to identify the scroll. I placed them as nearly as I had found them on the scroll under one of a number of 14-inch square panes of glass that the staff had also supplied in the lab. Other than that, they had placed an oil-burning stove near the door of the room. With a pen-knife I started working then on the main part of the scroll. The bottom of the scroll was black ebony, hard as ivory. It was clear that moisture in the cave over the two millenia it had lain there had caused the animal skin of one end of the scroll to disintegrate into mucous substance that then hardened into an ebony-like substance. This meant that a third of each column of the scroll was lacking. The full story of my experience opening the scroll is recounted in detail elsewhere.[1]

De Vaux had estimated that it would take six months to a year to get it totally unrolled, but the scroll was entirely under glass panes on the long table under those windows after only ten days coaxing it open, from November 10th to 20th, 1961. Najib Albina, a Palestinian Christian, was the

---

1. Sanders, "The Modern History of the Qumran Psalms Scroll and Canonical Criticism," in *Emanuel: Studies in Hebrew Bible, Septuagint, and Dead Sea Scrolls in Honor of Emanuel Tov,* edited by Shalom Paul, Robert A. Kraft, Lawrence H. Schiffman and Weston W. Fields with the assistance of Eva Ben-David (Vetus Testamentum Supplements 94; Leiden: Brill) 393–411.

photographer of the fragments and scrolls that had come in to the Palestine Archaeological Museum from all the sites discovered and/or excavated since John Trevor's photographs of the three scrolls from Cave 1 and those that Professor Sukenik had secured in 1948 on the Israeli side. Albina came to my room every morning I was working on the scroll, at about 11am when the sun shone best through the windows in the lab room, and took infra-red photographs of what I had done each day. He was excellent at his craft. After the Israelis had assumed responsibility of the PAM in 1967 they praised Albina's work as first-class, and it was.

Once the scroll was totally under glass I worked almost entirely with the Albina photographs. Because they were in infra-red the photos revealed more text to the naked eye than the scroll itself, and revealed it more clearly. Père de Vaux provided space for me in the library of the Ecole biblique where I worked through the winter and spring. Because the library of the Ecole biblique was/is one of the best in the world in biblical scholarship, and had an amazing, at the time unique, catalogue of all scholarly articles/papers published on each and every verse of the Bible, work on the scroll progressed rather rapidly. I was able by early January to send a preliminary report about the scroll to the *Bulletin of the ASOR* (*BASOR*) of which Prof. William F. Albright at Johns Hopkins University was editor. It was published the very next issue. Shortly thereafter I sent two articles about three psalms in the scroll that are not found in the traditional Masoretic (Hebrew) text of the Psalter to a journal in Germany.[2] Two of these were published before I arrived back home in Rochester. There I was enabled by my colleagues at CRDS to focus on working on the Scroll so that I was able to send a complete manuscript of my work on the scroll to Oxford University Press (OUP). It was published as *Discoveries in the Judaean Desert* (DJD), Vol. 4, in 1965. One cannot praise the Ecole biblique and its scholars enough who have over the years nurtured their fabulous library and its catalogues. Before I sent it off I took the working manuscript with me to visit Professors Cross at Harvard, Strugnell at Duke, and Skehan at Catholic University, who were gracious enough to work through the portions of the manuscript in their fields of expertise. Because of their careful scrutiny of what I had done the publication in 1965 met with considerable acceptance in the field and, in fact, has not had to be re-edited of all the volumes in the DJD series that have appeared—forty-two volumes total by 2002 of all the scrolls and fragments found in the Judaean Desert (the so-called Dead Sea Scrolls).

---

2. Sanders, "Psalm 151 in 11QPss," *Zeitschrift für die alttestamentliche Wissenschaft* 75 (1963) 73–86; and Sanders, "Two Non-Canonical Psalms in 11QPsa," *Zeitschrift für die alttestamentliche Wissenschaft* 76 (1964) 57–75.

— chapter 10 —

RACISM IN ROCHESTER

Back in the States the tensions about American Apartheid were brewing. A colleague at CRDS, William Hamilton, joined a group for a march in Alabama to protest the patent racism of the South with which I was well acquainted. When he returned to Rochester he wrote an op-ed article for the Sunday edition of the local paper, *The Democrat and Chronicle*, in which he made clear that he did not join the march to criticize racism there from a northern, self-righteous stance, but went to learn how to deal with racism in Rochester. The article so infuriated the publisher of the paper that he drove downtown that Sunday afternoon and wrote a rebuttal defending Rochester's history of "good relations" with blacks. He pointed out that after all Rochester was the home of Frederick Douglass, the founder of the Underground Railroad, and Walter Rauschenbusch, founder of the social gospel of Christianity. Bill, however, made his point very well and the next year Rochester experienced "riots" such as it had never imagined would happen in such a splendid city. Responsible civic and religious leaders of the city organized a response to the protests and invited a well-known community organizer from Chicago, Saul Alinsky, to come to Rochester to help work on solutions to its problems.

Rochester it turned out was as racist as the town in Alabama. The masthead slogan of Frederick Douglass' *The North Star* should still be heralded as a major message for the USA: "Right is of no Sex—Truth is of no Color—God is the Father of us all, and we are all Brethren."

It was truly difficult for most Rochesterians to grasp the truth that its proud, white population was basically racist. And yet when an official at Kodak at its head offices on State Street was approached about it, he seriously replied that Kodak had only so many floors to sweep. It was inconceivable to the gentleman or to most of Rochester that it simply did not know anything about its black citizens. But as the 1960s bore down upon them they slowly recognized that they were blind to the evil all around them. Even when I spoke with one of my liberal colleagues at CRDS about what Kodak could do his response became personal, "You don't know what you are talking about." He had studied for his doctorate at Harvard under the famous philosopher, Alfred North Whitehead. Others who had their PhDs from the University of Chicago were as ignorant of blacks and they grew almost as defensive of Rochester as the newspaper publisher. One wonders what Frederick Douglass would have said about Rochester's racism at the time.

Upon our return from Jerusalem to Rochester that fall I received an invitation to speak to the University Club of San Francisco about my experience with the scroll. I knew immediately that it had come indirectly from the Scroll's donor, Elizabeth Hay Bechtel, who lived in SF. I flew to California to meet her and her friends and to speak to the Club. She invited a number of her SF friends, among the elite of the city, to a reception in her apartment on Nob Hill. I had never seen a sight to match the view from her windows onto the bay where I saw the famous fog crawl in on "cat's paws." This was the first of numerous visits with Mrs. Bechtel. She came to visit us in Rochester and always brought with her very thoughtful gifts for Dora and Robin. Betty Bechtel was a very generous friend.

—chapter 11—

THE SIX-DAY WAR

In the summer of 1964 I was invited to teach in the summer session at Union Theological Seminary (UTS) in New York City. During the course of the summer I saw from time to time faculty (white men) sitting in for a session. I had no idea who they were at the time because they were scholars in fields other than mine. Then back in Rochester in 1965 a colleague, Charles Nielsen, burst into my classroom one morning just as the bell rang at the end of the hour, and grinning from ear to ear said in a loud whisper that Prof. Wilhelm Pauck had called and wanted to talk with me. I knew Pauck's name because he had been a professor of Nielson's at Union where Charley had gotten his doctorate. Pauck invited me down to Union for an interview about a position that would be open at the end of the year when Prof. James Muilenburg began retirement. After meeting with then Union president John Bennett and asking some questions Dora and I felt were important for us as a family I accepted Union's invitation to be professor of Old Testament beginning that fall. Dora would be going back to New York City where she had practically grown up and where she had frequently gone from Rochester to study in the various schools of modern dance and ballet, including Julliard which at that time was located on upper Broadway across 122nd Street from Union where the Manhattan School of Music is now located. I would be professor of Old Testament at Union Theological Seminary, which was about the highest honor one could receive in my field in the country. In August we took up residence in McGiffert Hall, apartment 702, on the Union campus. It had been the Muilenburg's apartment and was more than ample for us with four bedrooms, three baths, a dining room, kitchen, and library. The large living room looked north toward the George Washington Bridge and east toward Jewish Theological Seminary across the street on Broadway. In fact, for New York City it was palatial and was to be our home for the next twelve years.

I had met only a few faculty members outside biblical studies before opening exercises in September so that the grand occasion was very significant for me. The most meaningful new colleague was the Harry Emerson Fosdick Visiting Professor for the year, Abraham Joshua Heschel, professor of Jewish philosophy at Jewish Theological Seminary across the street on Broadway. I had read a few of his books, especially *The Sabbath* (1952) and *The Prophets* (1962), and admired his work tremendously. We found ourselves next to each other in the procession and that was the beginning of a friendship that would last until Heschel's untimely death on December 24th 1972. My office the first couple of years at Union had been Reinhold Niebuhr's office during the many years he had been professor of ethics at Union, and Heschel's office for the year was next to mine. Heschel used the Union office for the entire year. He kept the door open nearly all day for students or anyone at Union to come in for a visit. He was very generous with his time, and extremely generous with his time and wisdom to this young, new professor. We started at his suggestion a practice of going walking afternoons to get a little exercise and fresh air. We'd walk along either side of upper Broadway or on Riverside Drive just to the west. We continued this practice for the time we lived in New York until his death.

We'd take a few steps and stop and talk, another few steps and again stop and talk. One day we were on Broadway in front of Hastings Hall when I spotted our son, Robin, on his bike waiting patiently for a chance to interrupt us. But Heschel, who did not see Rob, didn't stop for quite a while so Rob left. I thought it good for Rob to show his respect for Heschel and wasn't worried about it. I knew that if what Rob had to say was truly important he would have waited and spoken up, but he didn't. That evening at supper Rob didn't say what he'd had in mind but instead asked why Heschel and I always seemed to be leaving synagogue and not going to it. I was so proud I could hardly mask it. Rob remembered that I'd told him that an observant Jew hastened to get to synagogue (*schul*) but walked reluctantly away after services. Next I saw Heschel I proudly told him what Rob said. Heschel was of course pleased but also concerned that Rob had not spoken up and interrupted him.

The first two years on the Union faculty I spent trying to convince myself that I truly belonged there. The faculty was star-studded with internationally renowned scholars including Paul Tillich, John MacQuarrie, Daniel Day Williams, Wilhelm Pauck, Cyril Richardson, Paul Lehmann, Hans Hoekendyck, Samuel Terrien, W. D. Davies, and others of similar fame. When word got around that I was to be Muilenburg's successor at

Union I got a handwritten note from Prof. John Strugnell (then at Duke, later at Harvard) asking me to remember him when I entered into my kingdom, paraphrasing the plea of the "good thief" to Jesus on the cross. Professor Strugnell had been especially helpful in scrutinizing parts of the manuscript I was preparing in 1962–63 to send to Oxford University Press to be published in the DJD series.

Mrs. Bechtel had requested that I prepare a second volume on the Psalms Scroll that lay folk could read and understand, so I spent considerable time in a carrel in the Union Library working up a manuscript for such a book. Detweiler suggested that the Cornell University Press would be glad to publish it, and they did in 1967.[1] I did my best in writing the second book to make the Scroll accessible to lay folk, but I also used the occasion to answer some of the critiques and reviews that early articles in journals and the Oxford University Press volume had incurred. She expressed her appreciation for the book when published but I don't think she cared much for the scholarly dimension of it. On the other hand, I have been told by close colleagues that the scholarly world has paid little or no attention to the Cornell edition since they thought it was solely for a lay readership.

Mrs. Bechtel and I frequently talked about the need to secure photographs of all the Dead Sea Scrolls in a protected vault outside the Near East. Tension was growing again in the area in early spring of 1967 when Mrs. Bechtel and I decided it was time to go out again to Jerusalem and see what could be done to fulfill our dream of preserving images of the Scrolls. We arrived in Jordanian Jerusalem in early May and went directly to the American School where we were able to stay in rooms in the hostel. We had several conversations with Père deVaux and other authorities. The problem was mainly the authorities in Amman who did not have much interest in our mission because the growing hostilities in the area commanded their attention. Gamal Abdul Nasser, the president of the United Arab Republic anchored in Egypt but including Syria, threatened to mine the Tiran Straits into the Gulf of Akaba, and hence to the Israeli port of Eilat, and made other sabre rattling threats against Israel. The Western scholars in East Jerusalem found it hard to take him seriously because we were well acquainted with Arabic hyperbole intended for home consumption, but war clouds were steadily gathering. We were particularly doubtful that he'd mined the Straits or would even finally do so. Most Western archaeological institutes in Jerusalem fell on the east side of the divide created when a truce was declared in 1948 after Israel had declared its independence and created a Jewish state. The French, British, German and American archaeological schools were/are

---

1. Sanders, *The Dead Sea Psalms Scroll* (Ithaca, NY: Cornell University Press, 1967).

all in East Jerusalem, and in conversations among ourselves we figuratively "bet" that if a war did break out Israel would win it within two weeks, so all of us expats in the old city went about business as usual. We knew that Nasser was engaging in typical Near Eastern rhetoric meant for consumption by Arabs in the area, and as it turned out he indeed had not mined the Straits.

When war did start on June 6th we began to hustle to exit Jerusalem over to Amman. I made sure that Mrs. Bechtel got out and was safely out of harm's way, and I then joined a group organized by Prof. John Mark of Princeton to drive the ASOR command car across the Jordan over to Amman. One of the vivid memories of the trip down into the Jordan Valley from Jerusalem was seeing out the back of our car an Israeli shell hitting the tower of the Lutheran hospital up on the east side of the Mount of Olives that the Israelis evidently suspected of being occupied by Jordanian troops. In Amman I met with Mrs. Bechtel to make sure she had flights home. I eventually flew to Beirut where I again visited with friends at the French Archaeological Institute and then flew on to Rome where I visited with Abbé Józef Milik who was in residence there at the time.

— chapter 12 —

Abraham Joshua Heschel

After I arrived home in New York I got a call from Kyle Haselden, editor of the *Christian Century* in Chicago, who asked me if I'd write up my experience. I agreed and he published it in mid-July initially titled "Urbis et Orbis: Jerusalem 1967."[1] The title was a take-off on the title of the Pope's annual address, Urbi et Orbi, "to Rome and to the world," but in the Latin genitive, "Of the City and the World," instead of the papal vocative. In the article I reviewed the five modes thus far suggested for the administration of Jerusalem and opted reluctantly for its being made an international city, like Trieste or Tangiers.

The article precipitated some of the most biting comments I have ever received from anyone. My friend, Prof. Yigael Yadin, probably the foremost archaeologist in Israel and a general of the Israeli division that had taken Jerusalem, sent me a telegram expressing his "dismay" on reading the article. Professor H. L. Ginsburg of the Jewish Theological Seminary across the street came over, pounded on my door and yelled at me that I did not deserve to be in "this office," which he knew had been Reinhold Niebuhr's. My view was that I indeed had followed Niebuhr's political philosophy in trying to look at all sides of an issue (Niebuhr was a true monotheizer) while Ginsburg remembered only Niebuhr's support of the founding of the State of Israel in 1948.

But the fall-out from the article was not seeing my mentor, Heschel, for several months to come. I learned from my wife, who was a close friend of Heschel's wife, that Heschel was writing a book about the "miracle" of the Six-Day War. He titled it *Israel: An Echo of Eternity*. I knew that Israel's victory was

1. Sanders, "Urbis and Orbis: Jerusalem Today," *Christian Century* 84/30 (July 26, 1967) 967–70.

not a miracle but fully expected despite the fact that the Jewish community in New York had been scared and deeply feared that Israel would be "pushed into the sea." I was frankly astounded to learn of that on my return. It was a sad example of how the same event can be understood totally differently by two distinctly different groups. It reminded me of the survey taken in 1925 after the nation-wide broadcast of the famous debate between Clarence Darrow and William Jennings Bryan after the Scopes Trial in Dayton, Tennessee: folk in the South almost unanimously hailed Bryan as the winner of the debate and folk in the North felt that Darrow had won hands down. Believing the victory in the Six-Day War to be a *neis* (miracle) was the substitute needed in the face of the fact that Messiah had not arrived. Many Jews began to believe because of the *neis* that they lived in a "messianic era," and that sufficed for most as the signal to accept fully politicized Zionism.

I didn't see Heschel for several months until late that fall when I ran into him coming out of the Union Seminary bookstore. I simply said, "Heschel, we've got to talk." That marked the end of our months-long period of silence. He had read my article and I his book. We resumed our walks and remained close friends until his death in December 1972. Occasionally on our walks we touched on our difference. One time when we were walking along Broadway opposite St. Paul's Chapel in the Columbia campus at about 118th Street, I mentioned that I'd read David Flusser's recent book, *Jesus*, and I was disturbed that Flusser read the NT text as though it were pure history and paid no attention to NT (literary and historical) criticism. Heschel remarked that he had the experience of speaking in churches and that he couldn't criticize Jesus. That was not what I meant at all, but I dropped the subject except to respond that I had the same experience in that I couldn't criticize the State of Israel! I met him on his own ground, and that brought us to leave that subject totally aside in future.

Once I did share with him how surprised I was that people in New York, especially Jews, felt that the Six-Day War was "a miracle" (in Hebrew a *neis*). He just looked at me as though I was from another world that I didn't know it was a miracle; his book that fall was based on the view that it was. Well, I had indeed just come from a different world—East Jerusalem and the West Bank—and knew that the one issue that unites the Arab governments of the area is enmity toward Israel which could not in any way make their united armies equal to Israel's.

A true miracle would be for Israel to befriend the Palestinian people. They have none as it is. No Arab government or people truly cares for the Palestinians as human beings. If Israel would re-assert its Jewishness, its true Jewish soul, and befriend the Palestinians as fellow human beings who worship the same One God of All, no matter the name either gives to God, it would find the security and safe haven Zionism sought in the first place. To continue for dubious reasons to seize and claim the homes and lands of Palestinians, that is, pursue its "manifest destiny" policies, will only increase the enmity not only of Arabs around the world but many others as well. Increasing the founding of "settlements" in the occupied West Bank exacerbates the enmity. If Israel instead would re-affirm the original early twentieth-century Zionist practice of being good neighbors to Palestinians the whole Near-East situation would shift to Israel's favor by taking away the principal reason Arab states have for hating Israel.

Sylvia Heschel, his widow and Dora's close friend, called us where we were in residence at the Ecumenical Institute at Tantur south of Jersualem to tell us that Heschel had died. It was Christmas Eve, December 24th, though no one mentioned that point. She later came to Jerusalem for Heschel's traditional Sheloshim (thirtieth day) service that was held at the Jewish Theological Seminary (JTS) Jerusalem campus. I had been invited to give one of the six speeches at the service, and it was a source of comfort that she was in the audience. My offering titled "An Apostle to the Gentiles" was well received and later that winter published in a JTS publication.[2]

That fall of 1967 marked the beginning of "student leadership" at Union and on Morningside Heights in general. The year before the "Columbia Bust," as it came to be called, students at Union, led by a handicapped student named Quigley, mounted a rebellion against Union's almost totally white, male faculty and against the very core of Reinhold Niebuhr's political philosophy that required appreciation of both sides in a conflict. The students were incensed at the injustices of the American war in Vietnam and at racism in America itself. They heard clearly the clarion calls of Eleanor Roosevelt (who to counter the Daughters of the American Revolution arranged to have Marian Anderson sing at the Lincoln Memorial on the Mall in Washington on Easter Sunday 1939), Martin Luther King, Jr. and of Union's own president, John Bennett, and of Abraham Heschel, in their resistance to racism and to the war, but they also wanted Union, despite its stellar reputation internationally to become more inclusive to represent at least the variety of backgrounds among the students themselves, including blacks and women. There were no blacks on the Union faculty at the time and only one woman, and she was in practical theology.

The Quigley Revolt, as it was called at Union, was a harbinger of the massive revolt centered the following spring at Columbia. How much the Columbia students were influenced by the earlier Union revolt was and still is not clear, but the protests were essentially the same. By April 1st, 1968,

---

2. Sanders, "An Apostle to the Gentiles," *Conservative Judaism* 28/1 (1973) 61–63.

students at Columbia were occupying the philosophy and mathematics buildings on the main campus at or near campus walk which was actually 116th Street between Broadway and Amsterdam Avenue. That night became brutal. Columbia had made plans to build a gymnasium on property it owned at the western edge of Morningside Park next to the Columbia campus along Morningside Drive, and the students seized on that plan to excoriate the Columbia administration and trustees for its near lack of minorities and women in faculty positions. Mayor John Lindsay, arguably the most liberal mayor New York City had had asked The Reverend Ernest Campbell if the New York Police Department (NYPD) could use the basement parking facility of The Riverside Church, arguably the most liberal Protestant church in the country, as a staging area for the mounted police of the NYPD. The Columbia campus was only a block away.

There were three student groups active that night: the rebelling students who occupied the buildings and were otherwise keeping the campus alert to the issues of the protest; the conservative jocks or student athletes who were preventing sympathizers from getting food and other supplies to the students inside the buildings; and the "Sundial People," a rather small group of graduate students and younger faculty, Reinhold Niebuhr activists one might say, who were trying to get a conversation going between the two opposing groups of students, and with the administration, to get them to hear each other and to try to resolve the tension by dialogue. The Sundial People were also "monotheizers," those who try in any situation, no matter how critical/crucial, to love the enemy, that is, ask "Why" each side of a conflict does what it does. The latter two groups are not often mentioned even in so-called histories of the events, just the rebelling students who, of course, were making the most noise and making the basic problem clear from their perspective, and the administration. The mounted police at one point mistook the Sundial People for rebelling students and many were injured by nightsticks in the attack.

The Sundial Group, of which I counted myself a member, were just as concerned about the lack of inclusion on the faculties of Union and Columbia as were the so-called rebels. They were convinced also, however, by the philosophy of Niebuhr that dialogue and compromise were the constructive way forward out of any conflict. They were also the "monotheizers," who according to this writer were obeying the most salient and first of all biblical commandments, including those of Jesus, to understand all sides of all conflicts. But when I attended rallies of students I heard only opprobrium against such an approach. We were, they claimed, "custodial liberals" and just as bad as Mayor Lindsay and The Reverend Campbell. Actually our group was as disturbed by what Lindsay and Campbell were doing as the rebelling students. We wanted instinctively the same results as the students but without the shouting and efforts to silence the other side.

Some faculty on both sides of Broadway (Columbia, Union and Barnard) found themselves locked out of their offices. The rebelling students did not want "scholarship as usual" to continue while they were putting themselves on the line for what they felt was right and just. Classes at Union were disrupted but continued as well as possible. Union's president, John Bennet, accused me of "egging" the students on. I was astounded when he said that. I responded that, on the contrary, I was teaching the Prophets the same way I had for fourteen years and that it was Amos and Jeremiah perhaps who egged them on, not I! Union's entering class in 1968 was the largest in its history. A few of the young men who matriculated admitted to me personally that by entering a seminary they were attempting to avoid the draft and being sent to Vietnam but were open to some form of ministry if not that of becoming pastors. Union had for most of its history been open to students who wanted to learn about Christian history, ethics and tradition as well as the best of biblical studies and Christian theology through the ages but who intended to take that knowledge with them into entirely different professions, not the church. We were used to that at Union and did not feel we were aiding and abetting "draft dodgers," as some of the Union trustees felt we were.

We soon learned that many other campuses experienced the same kind of protests, even in Europe, in the same time frame. Joseph Cardinal Ratzinger, who had been a professor in the Catholic Faculty at Tübingen University in Germany, was locked out of his office at Tübingen about the same time as the Columbia Bust. In personal conversation with Fr. Ratzinger when I was invited in September 1999 to read a paper at a conference in the Vatican sponsored by the Curia he was heading, he admitted that that experience turned him from a typical liberal in support of Pope John XXIII's understanding of Vatican II to being an active conservative in the church. Not only did he thereafter, during the papacy of John Paul II, become head of the Curia (the Congregatio Pro Doctrina Fidei) but eventually became his successor as Pope Benedict XVI.[3] Apparently some faculty here and in Europe did not hear Muhammed Ali's famous retort to a claim that he was letting his country down by not enlisting during the Vietnam War: "The Vietcong never called me nigger, and the Vietcong never tried to lynch me, so why should I go try to kill them?" Ali's stance against the Vietnam War was a serious indictment of America's attempts at playing global umpire.

3. Sanders, "Scripture as Canon in the Church," in *L'Interpretazione della Bibbia nella Chiesa* (Atti e documenti 11; Rome: Libreria Editrice Vaticana, 2001) 121–43.

— chapter 13 —

THE HEBREW OLD TESTAMENT
TEXT PROJECT

Back at Union the events of 1967–1968 caused a rather major change in faculty. Some of its faculty agreed with the trustees that the administration at Union and its faculty had abdicated responsibility during the protests and started leaving for other institutions. Others felt that the Union administration under John Bennett had failed to deal firmly with the situation. Some of the most prominent names on the faculty had left Union by 1970. All they'd had to do, I'm sure, was let it quietly be known that they were available. I personally wanted to continue at Union and witness some of the necessary changes to come, the main reason I turned the invitation to Yale University down in January 1970. Because of the large, nay huge, classes we had in those days, especially in the required courses, President Bennett found the money to hire young faculty to help. We hired Lloyd Bailey, who had just got his PhD, to help with the Old Testament load of classes. We made it very clear, or I thought we had, that those who came on the faculty in those positions were to stay only three years, and when the time came I counseled Bailey to accept a position that was open to him at Duke University Divinity School. The young man hired on the same terms for New Testament had also to leave but was accepted on the faculty of Auburn Seminary, a part of Union since the 1930s, so he could continue teaching at Union. I felt somewhat betrayed because I would very much like to have kept Bailey also, but felt constrained by the original agreement. Interestingly, one of the faculty brokers of student power worked through the students to keep the NT instructor (both white males). He and another faculty member had proved quite adept at playing the role of broker of student power in those days and was instrumental in my decision later on (in 1977) to leave the Union faculty. I was after all male, white, saw two sides to most issues, and quite dispensable—in their view.

The white brokers of student power made life miserable for those of us who worked for meaningful dialogue. When President John Bennett announced his desire to retire I, in the fall of 1969, was appointed chair of the faculty ad hoc committee to find a new president. One of the brokers was on the committee and a candidate whom he openly sponsored seemed to me a good choice—at first. When, however, I looked more closely into his credentials I changed my mind and paid for it dearly. The broker maneuvered a meeting of the full trustees committee to vote for his candidate at which I abstained from voting. I was tempted by then to vote No, but felt that I owed it to the candidate I had earlier sponsored at least to abstain. The otherwise unanimous vote by the trustee committee infuriated some of the more senior faculty. One of them summoned me to his apartment after the vote and laced me up and down without himself asking what my personal experience in the matter had been. I left his apartment stunned and baffled. I did not return to our apartment (in the same faculty building) but left campus walking pensively, trying to regain some sanity and composure. I walked blindly, as it were, and found myself, as my mind cleared, over on Amsterdam Avenue near the main Columbia Campus Walk, not remembering how I'd got there.

It was not long after that experience in December that I received an invitation from the Yale University Divinity School (YDS) to succeed the professor in the Winkler Chair there. I went up to New Haven twice and enjoyed the visits considerably, the second and last with my wife. Driving home late that January we stopped off at a restaurant on the Connecticut shore that we had always enjoyed and there, while dining, decided to stay at Union. I still am not sure it was the right decision, but Dora had made herself quite clear that she did not want to leave New York, and I was not sure I wanted to leave myself—except that I was so hurt by unfolding events at Union that I knew I wanted to leave when it was right. But a major factor that made me decide not to go to YDS came when I observed while there that the YDS faculty was as male and white as Union's had been, and I certainly did not want to engage in those battles again so soon. Actually Yale has never had a such rebellion but has slowly attempted to integrate its faculty.

I was invited in 1969 by the United Bible Societies (UBS) in Stuttgart to join a group with five others to form a research team to work on passages in the Hebrew Old Testament difficult for national translation committees around the world to translate. The UBS Translations Department under Eugene Nida had earlier formed a team of NT scholars in the 1950s to produce aids for NT translation committees, including the *Greek New Testament* (UBS, 1966), and he was launching a similar research team for the OT.

We began work in 1969 and completed the basic work in 1980. We met each summer in Freudenstadt in southwest Germany for a month to tackle problems passed on to us from UBS members who compiled lists of problems needing clarification according to the latest scholarship. The UBS, under Nida, was trying to reform its traditional mode of providing translations of the Bible into non-colonial languages, but the nationals recruited in the various countries around the world to work on the translations were less than well prepared to translate Hebrew and Greek biblical texts. They did what many ancients did who consulted standard early well-known Greek translations of the OT and inserted those meanings into Syriac and other ancient translations. Our task was to provide solutions to such difficult passages that the newly formed national translation committees could use in translating the biblical texts into their local languages.

I was the only American on the team. We had two from Germany, one from France/Switzerland, one from the Netherlands, one form the UK, and myself.[1] Each of us had assignments to work up each winter to share when we met each August/September. My responsibility was to provide all the readings from as yet unpublished Dead Sea Scrolls. Out of our work we agreed to publish the results of the 6000 passages we worked on in five volumes, and to work up for publication all the necessary data for a new, fifth edition of the Biblia Hebraica series the first of which had been published by the Deutsche Bibelgesellschaft back in 1905.[2]

1. Sanders, Review of *Biblia Hebraica Quinta: Fascicle 18: General Introduction and Megilloth*, Adrian Schenker, et al., eds. (Stuttgart: Deutsche Bibelgesellschaft, 2004) in *Review of Biblical Literature* (Atlanta; SBL, 2006) 1–10.

2. The fifth volume of Dominique Barthélemy's *Critique textuelle de l'Ancien Testament* has now appeared in the Orbis Biblicus et Orientalis series published by the Academic Press Fribourg/Vandenhoeck & Ruprecht Göttingen, 2015. Seven fascicles of the result of this work have so far been published as *Biblia Hebraica Quinta*, Nos. 1, 5, 7,13, 17, 18 and 20 by the Deutsche Bibelgesellschaft in Stuttgart.

—chapter 14—

SOUTH AFRICA

In September 1973 I joined a group of thirteen other Presbyterians in South Africa (SA), in response to an invitation from the Dutch Reformed Church of SA, to debate certain portions of the Presbyterian Confession of Faith published in 1967. I flew directly from our UBS session of 1973 in Freudenstadt, Germany, to Johannesburg to join the other Presbyterians for the debate with the SA church. The South African leaders of that church and of SA itself were disturbed by the Confession, especially its emphasis on racial equality. They felt it Communist and not Christian! When we arrived I felt I had been transported back to the Memphis of my youth. Segregation was total throughout the country. They called it Apartheid, or separate development. They were at least honest enough not to call it "separate but equal," as was the case in the US, where like in SA it was indeed separate but not all equal. The doctrine of Apartheid recognized that they were not equal but might eventually separately develop into equality—a pipe dream to support Apartheid. The whole time we were there I felt deeply uneasy at having to face again the truth of racism in my own country.

Shortly after returning from South Africa I was awarded my first honorary doctorate by Acadia University in Wolfville, Nova Soctia. I was proud that both my wife and our teenage son, Robin David, were with me for the occasion. Rob liked the Acadia situation so much that he spent his first two years of college there.

In 1989 I was invited again to SA, this time to be a visiting professor during the winter semester, July to early September, at the Stellenbosch University Theological Seminary, where I gave lectures on the Dead Sea Scrolls and their effect on biblical theology and where I worked with Prof. Johan Cook, their professor of OT, on the Scrolls. Dora went with me for the whole semester and they provided us a nice apartment as well as a comfortable stipend. Apartheid was still the rule of the land, but the Western policy of disengagement and boycott of SA was clearly having its effect. The Rand, the currency of the land, had become almost worthless outside the country. The apartment had a television set on which we were able to witness the campaign for who was to succeed P. W. Botha as prime minister. The Conservative Party candidate, F. W. de Klerk, would win without question since only whites could vote in the election. He did indeed win, but no one could have predicted what he did after the elections, which was to release Nelson Mandela from prison on Robben Island and meet him in Switzerland to work out a plan for integration of the government and set up new elections. Mandela, of course, was elected on the new plan and executed one of the most truly equalitarian and integrated constitutional governments in the world, with a Peace and Reconciliation program that soothed the whites' fears of retaliation. Back home conservatives had argued that boycotting SA would hurt the blacks more than the whites. The conservatives were again wrong as they have been throughout most of human history, but that of course has not prevented them from continuing to "conserve" inequality and injustice where it prevails.

While in SA in 1989 I had a wonderful visit with Archbishop Tutu at Bishops Court, the official residence of the archdiocese. Because I'd had moral struggles in myself as to whether I should accept the invitation to be a part of the Stellenbosch Seminary community for a semester I finally agreed to accept if the Stellenbosch faculty would help me secure an audience with Bishop Tutu while there. They actually did nothing to help, so I sought and procured an audience after I got there. I was driven one afternoon by the archbishop's chaplain to Bishop's Court. Tutu was not there, but Mrs. Tutu received me graciously and we had a friendly conversation in the garden where the sun warmed us on a chilly winter day. Mrs. Tutu was concerned that Tutu had not yet arrived because on the previous day while Tutu was at St. Mary's Church in Capetown the SA police gas-bombed the church which was holding an integrated meeting. The SA chief of police was Adrian Vlock, the notorious enforcer of Apartheid. The relief that showed on Mrs. Tutu's face when her husband arrived was a reflection of divine glory itself. The archbishop and I had a very warm and instructive interview before I was driven back to Stellenbosch.

After the semester concluded, Dora and I went to a private wildlife park called Tshukudu Park near Kruger Park. We had a marvelous experience there including walking with Shumba, an eleven-month-old lion. Shumba even invited himself at one point to join us for dinner on the porch of the lodge where he gulped down a steak of one of the guests! As usual the only blacks we saw were those that worked at menial jobs around the Park. At an earlier meeting with some professors one of them bragged about how big Kruger Park was. He claimed that it was so large it could contain within its bounds the whole of the State of Israel. I suggested that I thought that was a good idea. He was not amused and said SA had enough problems as it was. Indeed.

— chapter 15 —

UNION SEMINARY'S FUTURE

Meantime among the best things that happened to and at Union as a result of the changes taking place in the 1970s was hiring James Cone as professor of theology and Cornell West as professor of ethics. Some of the best thoughts about Union in those days that remain with me are the fact that I labored hard to get these two brilliant theologians on the Union faculty before I left. Cone is still on the faculty and West returned after having served on Harvard and Princeton faculties in the interval. One of the moments that I shall forever cherish occurred when West came to speak to the Adult Forum at All Saints Episcopal Church in Pasadena where I had been invited to speak several times myself. As I made my way to the Forum meeting, West came over and hugged me warmly and then during his presentation addressed me as "Brother Jim Sanders." I will always cherish that moment. It marked for me a climax of my conversion from being a born-again bigot to being called out as a brother of Cornell West. A similar experience occurred in 1990 at All Saints Church when Archbishop Tutu was invited to preach. Tutu had often preached at All Saints, but this time it was nearly a year after I had had the privilege of visiting with him at Bishops Court in Capetown. Several students drove me over to Pasadena to hear him, but because of the crowds we had to sit outside the church in chairs set up near where the procession would pass. As Tutu passed our chairs he spotted me and broke out of the procession, came over to where we sat and embraced me warmly. That was a moment, like the one with Cornell West, and later a telephone call from Gardner Taylor just before he died, that will remain in my heart as long as it beats. If a request could be granted it would be to have a place with my dear wife alongside those three when Gabriel's trumpet sounds.

Another factor, probably the crucial one, in my decision personally to stay at Union at the time was the fact that at Union we were in the
throes of inviting a world-renowned NT scholar to come to Union as part
of the agreements to co-operate with a Jesuit seminary that would move
to Morningside Heights to work jointly with Union. Raymond E. Brown
was not Jesuit. He was actually Sulpician, but that was basically meaningless because he was the kind of NT scholar I wanted to work with. Brown
and I had a delightful time working up in our minds a doctoral program in
biblical studies that focused on the causes for the rise of Judaism out of the
Babylonian Exile in the sixth century BCE that thereafter developed into
the multi-faceted Hellenized Judaism (or Judaisms, as some have said) out
of which Christianity arose and developed. In the middle of the negotiations
with Yale I was invited to lecture at the Acadia University Divinity School
in Nova Scotia. While there I got a phone call from Brown, while he was
still at St. Mary's in Baltimore, in which he made it clear that if I stayed at
Union he would come—if not, he would not. That did it. When we arrived
back from New Haven after our second trip up there I called John Bennett,
still president at that time, and told him we would stay. I had made Brown's
coming as a condition for staying. We were both made Auburn Professors
of Biblical Studies at Union Seminary.

I had not taken a sabbatic leave since I arrived at Union in 1965 and
therefore had a full-year due. I applied for and received a second Guggenheim Fellowship to enable me to accept an invitation to be one of the two
first Senior Fellows at the Ecumenical Institute for Advanced Theological
Study that had just been constructed north of Bethlehem on property do-
nated by Pope Paul VI. The pope had visited Jerusalem soon after the 1967
Six-Day War and there decided to institute such a center as a result of the
ecumenical dimension of the Second Vatican Council that had taken place
in Rome under Popes John XXIII and Paul VI (1962–1965). The other Senior Fellow had been my NT teacher in Paris, Oscar Cullman. It was a great
honor to be associated with Cullman in this manner.

Robin David, our son, had just turned seventeen in September of
1972 when we arrived at Tantur, the Arabic name of the hillock just north
of Bethlehem where the Institute is located. Dora and I flew over, but Rob
sailed in a freighter first-class so he could bring his bicycle over with him.
He registered at St. George's secondary school in Jerusalem to take courses
while we were there for the year. He rode his bike there and back from Tantur to the school every day that school year. Rob made friends with Arab
Christian and Muslim youth his age that year, an experience that has stayed
with him until now. Another friend he made was Tsafiris, a Greek Orthodox

young man in residence at Tantur, with whom Rob played ping-pong almost nightly that year. Tsafiris has since become a bishop in the Greek Church.

William Dever was director of the American School in Jerusalem and remained director for several years until he returned to the US to be professor at the University of Arizona. The spring of 1973 Bill and Norma, his wife, returned for a month to the States. During that time, he asked me to be acting director in his place while he was away. I was on the board of trustees of the ASOR corporation at that time. Dora, Rob, and I moved into the quite ample Director's Apartment on the campus of the ASOR in Jerusalem for the month. It was during that month that Dora was hired as pianist for classes at the Rubin Academy of Music and Dance in West Jerusalem, and she remained so through the Yom Kippur War that fall after Rob and I returned to the States.

That was the last of the six halcyon years after the Six-Day War of 1967 during which Jerusalem and the whole of Palestine was open for travel for everyone—Israelis, Palestinians, pilgrims, and visitors. One passed freely and without hindrance from one side to the other. Those six years stand out in my mind as model for how it can and should be now and hereafter. But alas, the Yom Kippur War of the fall of 1973 changed all that.

When the semester started at Union in September of 1973 I re-entered the turmoil that the brokers of student power had created, only it was worse. I had to thank my close colleagues on the faculty for not writing me about the battles that had taken place during the year we were away, so that I had a truly peaceful and fruitful year in Jerusalem. When I saw what was happening after my return I consulted with several colleagues and instigated a petition that sought to halt further voting by the Union Assembly until real dialogue could take place. In the petition I called for theologizing about Union and its mission. I found that nearly all my colleagues, except for the three, wanted a breather and agreed with the petition. The principal broker, on the contrary, by launching a personal attack on me vilified the petition as a personal attack on him. He diverted the purpose of the petition by claiming it was a personal attack on him and his ability as a theologian. He was an accomplished manipulator. The diversion he sought succeeded and the Union Assembly (2/3 faculty and 1/3 students and staff) that had earlier replaced traditional faculty meetings voted the petition down. I was baffled and mystified that the faculty had been so cowed that it took my return from a year's leave to precipitate such an attack. Within two weeks of our return from Jerusalem my emotions were back to the turmoil they had been when we left. I soon had an invitation to return to San Francisco to give lectures and while I was there during a sleepless night—even nearly 3000 miles away

from Union—I resolved to leave Union. I also asked myself during that trip
if it had been right to turn down the invitation to Yale two years earlier.

After my return to New York from the West Coast, Eulalia Williams
called and asked me to come to their apartment, in our same building, because her husband, Daniel Day Williams, had fallen and she thought maybe
he'd broken a hip. I rushed down there and found Dan on his bed in considerable pain. We called an ambulance and I accompanied him and Eulalia
to St. Luke's Hospital near the Columbia campus on Amsterdam Avenue.
Another trip to the West Coast took place precisely during Dan's stay in the
hospital. I felt honored to get back in time to take Dan home. But only a few
weeks after that Dan fell again and Eulalia again called me down to their
apartment. While we were waiting for the ambulance to arrive I asked Dan
if he felt that maybe his falls were caused by the tension we all were living
with that autumn. He admitted that he wondered that himself. I didn't say
anything about the resolution I'd made while in San Francisco, that wouldn't
have helped Dan at that point.

Unfortunately on December 3rd, 1973, Dan died in the hospital from
an embolism while Eulalia was away from his side for only a short time to
do a bit of shopping. Eulalia never got over Dan's death and especially that
he died during the very short period of time she was away from his side. She
and Dora had been good friends because of their common interest in classical music, but after Dan's death they became very close and remained so
after Eulalia moved to Claremont's Pilgrim Place retirement community until her death. Dora was already a close friend of Sylvia Heschel's because of
their common interest in music, and that too would last until Sylvia's death.
We have both been close with Susannah Heschel, their daughter, nearly all
Susie's life, and that has continued to this very writing. Susie is a prominent
professor at Dartmouth College.

Not long after Dan's death, Dora and I came up with the idea of honoring the deaths of Abraham Heschel, who had died the previous December,
and of Daniel Williams, with a concert at Riverside Church of Braham's
German Requiem. In consultation with Ernie Campbell at Riverside, and
of Riverside's director of music and organist, Frederick Swann, we began
to organize the concert. Even though Sylvia Heschel was enthusiastic, in
an effort to draw Jewish Theological Seminary into the celebration I visited
with President Louis Finkelstein who gave us tepid support. I then called
Prof. Yohanan Muffs, a close friend at JTS, by phone. I told him of our plans
and our hope that he would join us in the attempt to honor our two colleagues. On the contrary, with great emotion Muffs shouted into the phone
that Heschel was not a Christian. This totally floored me. We had chosen
the Braham's Requiem precisely because it was non-Christian. There is no

mention of Christ or anything Christian in the Requiem. I quietly thanked
Yochie and rang off. I sat in my office slumped over utterly defeated. I called
Campbell and Eulalia and told them that JTS did not think well of the idea
and that we should cancel.

—chapter 16—

GARDNER TAYLOR
AND CONCORD CHURCH

For my sanity I in effect gave up on Union, and JTS for that matter. I ceded the battles. Though I did not myself say anything about Union's problems off campus, nor that I was available, I nonetheless got invitations from four internationally renowned academic institutions over the following year and a half. Two of these were in California, and I finally accepted the one from the School of Theology at Claremont (now the Claremont School of Theology—CST) in southern Calfornia near Los Angeles, with a joint appointment at the Claremont Graduate University. We moved to Claremont in 1977 and still live here even after retirement. Pilgrim Place, where many colleagues from both New York and Claremont live in retirement, is only a block from our home.

One of the ways I retained my sanity while still in New York was I gave up on the "white" churches in Manhattan. A part-time colleague at Union in homiletics, Dr. Gardner Taylor, was pastor of the Concord Baptist Church of Christ in Bedford Styvesant in Brooklyn. With urging from no one I attended services there Sundays for several years. Concord practiced a form of evangelical Christianity that soothed my soul and fed my spirit. It reminded me of my "born-again" experience in the tent on Third Street in old South Memphis. It was about as far from the current politicized evangelicalism as one can get. It is little wonder that Donald Trump appeals to white evangelicals because it gives them the justification to support the bogotry that the present Republican Party has sunk to.[1]

---

1. See Peter Whener, "The Theology of Donald Trump," *New York Times*, July 5, 2016. Whener was active in several Republican administrations.

Gardner, of course, recognized me from the first time I attended Concord Church and often would defer to me during his sermons. I chose a pew in the balcony just above the rostrum where Gardner preached and continued to occupy that same place for the time I attended Concord. I usually stayed after service for Sunday dinner at the church. Different groups of the church ladies prepared the delicious dinners. Dora teased me a bit saying she knew the real reason I went to church at Concord was the Southern cooking. It was indeed "down-home" cooking, and I loved it, but I went to church there because I truly appreciated Gardner's preaching as well as the genuine evangelical services he conducted and that I was indebted to from my youth. Most white evangelical churches, especially the Southern Baptists, are a travesty since Jerry Falwell politicized the movement in 1979 whereas black Protestant churches are a blessing not only for those who attend them but for the country as a whole.[2] Gardner, who was originally from Louisiana, was also part-time professor of homiletics at Harvard. In weather good and bad I took the Sunday *New York Times* with me on the A train out to Brooklyn each Sunday. I'd read about half of it on the trip out and the rest on the train coming home. One of the deacons of the church would take it and secure it somewhere for me and then return it when I'd leave. After dinner Gardner would celebrate communion ("The Lord's Supper") but make sure the good folk who stayed for it had time to get back home before dark and the dangers that readily lurked at the time in the streets of Bedford-Styvesant.

Gardner eventually retired from Concord Church to a retirement community in North Carolina. We stayed in touch sporadically, but in early December 2014 I received a call I'll never forget. It was from Gardner a few weeks before he died. I'm as sure as I can be about anything that Gardner made that call to say Good-bye, and I'm also as sure as I can be in this old world that I'll get to hear that golden-voice preach again in some other dimension of God's amazing creation. His call before he left us will stay with me like the times in years earlier when Cornell West and Bishop Tutu embraced me and called me brother. My heart will remain full of these memories until that other call eventually comes as it must for us all. Please God that I be permitted, when it does, to be assigned a position near theirs to sing the praises of the One who made us all and to pray fervently for the amazing but pitifully sinful human race.

Before we had gone out to spend the year at Tantur in 1972–73 my book *Torah and Canon* (1972) appeared. It went into 13 printings I was informed while it was still a title of Fortress Press, and it is still selling

2. Sanders, "The Betrayal of Evangelicalism"; see appendex below.

forty-three years later under the aegis of Cascade Books who published a Second Revised Edition in 2005. There have been several follow-up books that are also still in print. The book that has probably sold almost as well is *God Has a Story Too* (1979), a group of sermons I preached during the creative turmoil of the late 1960s and early '70s.

— chapter 17 —

Counseling LGBT Ministers

For some reason I have attracted students (I continue to teach in retirement) who need counseling about personal matters—students whose
marriages were on the shoals, students who were unsure about going into
ministry and yet needed to be registered in a seminary to avoid going to
some misbegotten war, students who needed to tell someone that they didn't
believe in God, and especially students who needed to share who they truly
were with a sympathetic ear but didn't dare tell others, especially authoritative figures. Among the latter have been a number of gay and lesbian students. Through most of my years of teaching (I am now in the 63rd) gay
students needed, before going into a church-related ministry, to tell somebody their life-long secret. I learned early on that being gay was clearly not
a choice. Some of my students in sheer agony come to ask how they could
continue to live their lie, yet be a minister. After I tell them that I personally
know of several ministers who are in the closet, I then ask them if being
in the closet is truly a choice for them. Gays know deep inside that being
homosexual is not a choice one makes, but they can choose whether to live
in the closet or come out and stop living the lie they are forced to live by
evangelical and other Christians who believe that God is locked inside the
Bible, especially in their readings (their hermeneutic) of it.

Gays and lesbians tell me how early in life (5 years old for some) they
knew it was a secret they had to keep or be rejected, especially by "religious" parents or friends. A few came to weep about how miserable it had
been to finally tell the truth. Some parents who claimed to be "Christian"
had disowned them and thrown them away, in fact, the parents said, it was
because they were "Christian" that they disowned their children because
the child had "chosen" her or his life style—utterly contradicting all the

79

scientific disciplines that address the issue of homosexuality because, they say, the Bible condemns it. They, of course, make no mention of the dozens of biblical injunctions they as evangelicals or Catholics totally ignore. They practiced and practice what Father Daniel Berrigan called "scrap-book biblical teaching." Such parents and their pastors are the ones who "choose," namely the mores of antiquity instead of modern science. It is they who do the choosing, not the young gay or lesbian. One has to ask why they choose to focus on homosexuality of all the biblical condemnations instead of on the many other "sins" some of which they themselves practice. It is a choice evangelical pastors especially force on their flocks in order to preserve what they perceive as the authority of the Bible, which in my view is that which exposes their ruinous abuse of the Bible as "The Word of God" instead of reading it as a select record of what God was able to do with people in and through ancient cultural mores and contexts. My students, by contrast, come to the kind of seminary in which they chose to study in order to try to find a measure of acceptance, by somebody, of who they really are, that is, a liberal seminary that believes in the teachings of Jesus who said not a word about gays one way or the other but who said we should love each other no matter what. But that does not suit the white evangelical support of the biases so many Americans practice. As Ramdall Balmer poignantly says, "Evangelicals are secular now . . . they have devolved from theological guardians to political operatives."[1] America harbors one of the most racist societies in the world.[2] I stress that God is not locked into the Bible nor its ancient metaphors in reference to God.[3] Politicized evangelicals are authoritative in another way as well. They like to cite Paul's Epistle to the Romans (13:1) which clearly admonished the church in Roman to obey secular authorities because they wouldn't be in charge if God did not want it. The passage did not seem to restrain them from opposing President Obama at will but provides Scriptural base (in their scrap-book Bible) for supporting President Trump no matter his quite un-Christian personal life. President Jerry Falwell of Liberty University replies that Trump is a baby Christian (echoing 1 Corinthians 3:1 and 1 Peter 2:2?).

It has been observed that everyone can be placed on a spectrum of sexuality from one to ten, as it were.[4] Some of us are straight who nonethe-

1. See Randall Balmer's "Evangelicals' Support of Trump," *Los Angeles Times*, March 3, 2016; and Elizabeth Dias' "Trump's God Machine," *Time* 187/22 (May 2016) 30–34.

2. See Nicholas Kristof, "When Whites Just Don't Get It," *New York Times*, April 2, 2016.

3. Note Carel van Schaik and Kai Michel, "Atheists and Believers are Reading the Bible the Wrong Way," *Los Angeles Times*, 10 June 2016.

4. See Jay Michaelson, *God vs. Gay? The Religious Case for Equality* (Boston: Beacon,

less have had sexual interest piqued in a person of the same sex. And some of us are gay who nonetheless have had sexual interest piqued in a person of the opposite sex. Most of us know who we are deep inside and live with it, perhaps repressing the occasional attraction in the other direction. Others are truly bisexual, about five on the spectrum. One observation I have made through the years is that those who are truly straight quite honestly cannot identify with a gay person's inclination, and, vice versa, those who are truly gay simply cannot imagine having sex with a person of the opposite sex. They know deep inside that they are turned off by the thought. On the other hand, another observation has been that the bisexual person, or the gay who has lived a lie in the closet since childhood, almost instinctively see two sides to many issues they face. They have for so long been forced by society to mask their true feelings that they automatically say what is expected of a "straight" pastor, yet inside immediately perceiving two sides to the issue and often perceive two sides to most issues, political, cultural and social.

I often suggest to such students that God had made them that way precisely because gay ministers often turn out, in my long experience of teaching and keeping in touch with alumni, to be the best ministers the churches have. Why? Because they of all the students can almost instinctively see two sides to issues, and not just issues of one's sexuality but most issues that humans face. I also would suggest that it placed a heavy burden on them to fulfill that mission. Gays who are forced by "religious," especially white, evangelical folk to live a lie know almost intuitively the misery of some of those who come to them because they know deep inside who they are but daren't tell anyone the truth. To some I even was able to say that gayness is a precious gift God gives to a favored few to minister to people that live in agony created by born-again bigots like myself—until my conversion to liberal Christianity, the form of Christianity that attempts to follow the teachings of Jesus as recorded in the Gospels. The work and experience of Glenn Greenwald comes to mind. Greenwald moved to Rio de Janeiro so he could live with his husband. Why? Because, he says, of the "Defense of Marriage" act by Congress. Greenwald is exceptional in the world of journalism (he won a Pulitzer Prize while with the *New York Times*) because he insists on asking "Why?" in any situation he investigates. It is unfortunately typical of most of us to demonize those we disagree with or at least make disparaging *ad hominem* remarks.[5]

2011) xiii–xxii.

5. See Glenn Greenwald, *With Liberty and Justice for Some: How the Law Is Used to Destroy Equality and Protect the Powerful* (New York: Metropolitan Books, 2011).

Whereas most people immediately condemn those who bomb our cities as terrorists and demonize them, the good guys, says Greenwald, ask why they bomb us. Our resolutions to get tough and respond in kind, he points out, only cause them to further resolve to hurt us as much as they can. It hasn't been only evangelicals who force gays to lie, the Marine Corps until a few years ago claimed that there were no gays in the Corps, a patent lie that has been forcefully exposed.[6]

In my thinking that makes Greenwald a monotheizer, he practices loving the enemy as a fellow Jew a couple of millenia ago taught so clearly (Matthew 5:43–48; Luke 6:27,35; cf. Proverbs 25:21 and especially Jeremiah 29:7).[7] Of course, the Old (or for Christians, First) Testament already arrived at the monotheizing process through the teachings of the ancient prophets of Israel and Judah.[8] I often find myself trusting Jewish political leaders in the USA to do what is just and right for all of us because if they grew up in Reform Jewish homes, as most American Jews do, they learned that the mission of Israel is to live lives of Torah out in the real world (and not in Ghettoes, even a nation-Ghetto) and to fight for truth and justice wherever they are. Unfortunately Reform Judaism has lost its way and become as Zionist (which is not the same as Jewish) as Conservative Jews. Even most Orthodox Jews, who originally opposed Zionism, have since 1967 confused the two. Conservative Judaism was founded in 1901 by Solomon Schechter to support Zionism because Orthodox and Reform Judaism did not. Now only a small remnant of Reform Jews still remember and practice the mission of Israel as Reform was founded to do.[9] And, of course, there will always be scattered Orthodox *schuls* who do not recognize the State of Israel. It would seem to me that one can and should recognize the State of Israel but that Israel itself should embrace the ideals of Reform Judaism, or at least the ideals of the original Zionist kibbutzim before the partition of Palestine, and encourage Israel to be the Palestinians' best friend. No Arab state represents the interests of the Palestinians who have sacrificed their homes to allow there to be an Israel. If there are a few rockets and rock throwings the true Jew will first ask why the Palestinian youth are angry enough to toss them. Are humans naturally reluctant to learn about themselves that they fail to ask why terrorists act as they do? It would be helpful to remember

6. See Justin Crockett Elzie, *Playing by the Rules* (Bar Harbor, ME: QueerMojo, 2010).

7. See Sanders, *The Monotheizing Process* (Eugene, OR: Cascade Books, 2014).

8. Sanders, "Hermeneutics of True and False Prophecy," in the Walther Zimmerli Festschrift: *Canon and Authority* (Philadelphia: Fortress Press, 1977), 21–41.

9. See the *The Reform Advocate* of the Society for Classical Reform Judaism, 15 Newbury Street, Boston MA 02116.

that the Irgun, the Hagganah, The Stern Gang, and other such (now called) "patriotic" groups were all condemned by the British as terrorists during the Mandate days before partition. In fact, one can go through history and find many such early groups who are/were later viewed as heroes were originally condemned as terrorist by the authorities of that time.[10]

10. See Ben Ehrenreich's *The Way to the Spring* (New York: Penguin, 2016) for a rare but sane perspective on the Israeli occupation of Palestine as it is today.

—chapter 18—

CLAREMONT

History, and especially recent history, shows how to love the enemy, but it usually has taken a half-century or more to reach that point. It has taken Southerners longer to accept the results of the Civil War than Northerners, but no one questions the principle of the Union of the USA as it was disastrously questioned by the rebellious Southern Confederacy. Two of the closest allies of the USA today, Germany and Japan, were mortal enemies 65 years ago; we called them Nazis and Japs. A little over a century ago anyone who took up the cause of native Americans was pejoratively called "Injun lover." The question is whether it is possible for humans to understand the hurt others experience at the time the hurt is inflicted. Must it take a half-century or more to love the enemy? One hopes that the sea-change in the attitude of most Americans toward blacks, homosexuals, and others who are different that has taken place in the last decades is a harbinger of the possibility that humans can love, if not enemies, at least those who are "others" in our society.

To monotheize is to ask why, the question hardly ever posed by those who instead demonize anybody that causes them pain. We should instead ask what pain we may have first caused them.

Occasional actions of justice on the part of the Supreme Court that drew the country closer to both the teachings of the prophets and of Jesus but also to the ideals of the eighteenth-century Enlightenment that produced the Declaration of Independence and the Constitution of the United States exposed, starkly to the country and the world the South's Jim Crow laws. But the USA was and still is far from the Enlightenment ideals on which it

84

was based.[1] These actions underscored the need the likes of the Reverend Martin Luther King, Jr., and of Rabbi Abraham Joshua Heschel, and indeed of secular forces in the country such as movies, television productions and commercials, exposed finally for the world to see.[2] They certainly were not due to the churches in the country; the latter were and still are for the most part the most segregated and hate-inspiring institutions in the country. It is by and large a farce to suggest that most churches in this country follow the teachings of Jesus. The endorsement of Donald Trump by evangelical leaders belies this point.

When we moved to Claremont, California, in 1977 I thought we'd find an environment closer to what America was supposed to be, and in some ways it was. But we were shocked to find de facto segregation alive and well in Claremont. Our first residence was in an apartment located in what we later learned was called "the love triangle," the residence of most of the blacks in the city. Blacks who had been able to move up the social and economic ladder found residence in other parts of our small city, but they were/are few indeed. We learned that until 1955 Claremont had a city ordinance forbidding blacks to be in the City after 9pm. Maids and other "help" often had to run to catch a bus to get out of Claremont in time not to be arrested. Well after the ordinance was repealed blacks are still shamed and repressed by officials and ordinary citizens. The Police Department of the city, it must be noted, has tried to curb black profiling but it has been slow and very late. As Arthur Ashe, the tennis great, suggested it might help if whites in positions of authority had to live and go about their regular routines for just a day they would learn what blacks in this country have to contend with.[3] Even black professionals often suffer humiliation because of American racism. As some tell me quietly they don't know what they'll face when they leave the sanctuary of their homes, or ours, on any given day. Even well-meaning whites trying to show how liberal they are treat blacks differently from the way they would treat a similar white person. They often seem more interested in showing their tolerance than in showing true citizenship toward blacks. It has become clear that objections by some to "political correctness" is in fact an attempt on the part of conservatives to stifle liberal efforts to bring the country more in line with the Constitution and with "the angels of our

---

1. See Matthew Stewart, *Nature's God: The Heretical Origins of the American Republic* (New York: Norton, 2014).

2. See Sanders, "God's Work in the Secular World," *Biblical Theology Bulletin* 37 (2004) 145–52.

3. See Arthur Ashe's personal experiences with American racism in his *Days of Grace: A Memoir* (New York: Knopf, 1993).

better nature," as President Lincoln sagely remarked.[4] The pejorative decry-
ing "political correctness" is clearly but an effort to protect tribal biases and
bigotry toward the "other" in society (violating Exodus 12:49; Leviticus
24:22; Numbers 9:16; 15:15; 16:29, etc.).

The principal reason for the move to Claremont was that my bene-
factress, Elizabeth Hay Bechtel, would not donate money in New York. She
had always been a Californian. Due to her and her husband Kenneth's generosity a number of Cave 11 Dead Scrolls materials were released for study
and publication, in addition to the Wadi ed-Daliyah papyri found further
north in Palestine in the late 1950s. I had been appointed to unroll and
study the large Cave 11 Psalms Scroll for publication and because of that
made Mrs. Bethtel's acquaintance. She befriended me and my family and
visited us when we lived in Rochester and then in New York City, often with
expensive gifts for our son, Robin, and for Dora. Mrs. Bethtel was keenly
interested in securing images of the Scrolls for posterity so that she and I
made a number of visits to Jerusalem to gain permission from the various
authorities there to make photographic copies of all the Scrolls for storage
outside the Near East in a safer place. Mrs. Bechtel's interest was in preservation while mine was broader. I wanted the Scrolls preserved in a safe
haven, for sure, but I also wanted to establish a place where images of all the
principal manuscripts on which the Hebrew and Greek texts of the two testaments of the Bible are based would be available to any and all competent
scholars in order to reduce the high number of errors often committed by
excellent scholars who simply did not have access to images of the originals
but had to depend on prior scholars' publications. Most Jews and Christians
do not realize that the scholarly editions used for study and translation into
English and other modern languages often contained errors copied from
earlier scholarly editions of the Hebrew and Greek testaments.

Mrs. Bechtel and I came to an agreement that would include both our
interests so that I accepted an invitation to join the faculties at Claremont
which was already well known for its interest in biblical and related ancient
texts. The founder of the School of Theology at Claremont (STC), Ernest
Cadmon Colwell, and James M. Robinson, the founder of the Institute for
Antiquity and Christianity (IAC) in Claremont, were both New Testament
scholars. She funded the building of a large wing on the Claremont School
of Theology library to house what we were to call The Ancient Biblical
Manuscript Center (ABMC)—with a state-of-the-art climatized vault in
which to preserve films of all the manuscripts we would be able to collect

4. See Aimée Liu's op-ed article in the *Los Angeles Times*, 27 March 2016: "Political
Correctness may have run amok, but it's better than when casual racism ruled." It still
rules; witness Donald Trump's many speeches during the election campaigns of 2016.

from all over the world. Mrs. Bechtel was generous to a fault if I agreed with her or supported her ideas, but she treated all of us dedicated to the mission of the ABMC as her employees. She had no other concept for us than that of employees. She was born into wealth and married into a family of fabulous wealth and had difficulty understanding how to relate to those she benefited.

— chapter 19 —

THE ANCIENT BIBLICAL
MANUSCRIPT CENTER

After she moved her residence from Santa Barbara to Claremont itself in May 1980 she came into the Center daily and constantly found fault with Peggy Woodruff, our faithful and highly competent office manager, and with my graduate students who gave of themselves unstintingly to make the Center work. From the moment she tried to run the Center herself in the summer of 1980 it became difficult to keep anyone on the staff. She had me fire three directors that summer. A friend of hers on the board tried to tell her saying, "Betty, Jim is living in a fish bowl with three dead fish," but she did not understand what he was saying. She had no way of recognizing criticism since she was hardly ever criticized in her whole life. She treated all of us as employees, the only way she knew to relate to us. It was beginning to affect me personally to the point that I told the Executive Committee in September that I could no longer work with Mrs. Bechtel. I was more than ready to sacrifice my dream in order to regain some sense of psychic health. Professor Frank Cross of Harvard, a member of the board, came down to Claremont to support me so that I decided to stay if Mrs. Bechtel stopped trying to run the Center herself.

Mrs. Bechtel, however, left the board of the ABMC in December of 1980 after commandeering the photos of the scrolls at the Los Angeles airport (LAX) and taking them to the Huntington Library for storage—all illegal moves, but she did not care since she could not conceive of herself doing anything wrong. But the ABMC nonetheless continued its acquisition of films of originals of ancient and medieval manuscripts housed in libraries and monasteries around the Western world. We mounted projects of sending photographic teams wherever we were welcomed. My own personal scholarly work suffered for the good reason of going about the country, accepting almost all invitations that came in to lecture on the Scrolls or on my work on the Bible as canon, to raise the money to keep the ABMC operating. Mrs. Bechtel created a story that suited her view of what happened including the accusation that I took over the ABMC in order to have access to all the Scrolls for my own benefit. The opposite was the truth. My work in scholarship suffered thereafter because of the burden of making the Center work. During the 23 years I was president of the ABMC Claremont gained an international reputation beyond even what it had previously had.

In 2003 I was invited out of the ABMC and Professor Marvin Sweeney was made CEO after which the mission of the Center was changed so that all such projects were dropped, including ones that we had worked on, through the valiant efforts of our last director, Michael Phelps, to photograph the invaluable collection of ancient manuscripts in the some 20 monasteries on Mt Athos in Greece and the incomparable collection in St Catherine's Monastery on Mt Sinai in Egypt. All that stopped when Phelps and I were invited out, so that Phelps thereafter established the Early Manuscripts Electronic Library (EMEL) to continue work on both those projects and more such projects since. Sweeney made no personal effort to raise money other than editing *The Folio*, the quarterly organ of the ABMC created in 1981 by Richard Weis and myself. He turned the ABMC into a "faculty center" which it had never been.

After I had been at Claremont for over seven years I took a long-overdue sabbatic leave the full year 1985–1986. I applied for a Rockefeller Foundation Grant to take up residence in the Foundation's fabulous Serbelloni castle on 55 acres of grounds in Bellagio, Italy. For a full month Dora and I lived like royalty while I worked away at a writing project in a private study that had been a free-standing guard house situated by a beautiful goldfish pond on the grounds of the castle. We went on from there to take up residence for a second time at the Ecumenical Institute at Tantur north of Bethlehem, but this time for one semester only. The second semester I returned home where I was able to work full time on the book I'd started at Bellagio that would appear three years later. The book received warm praise from most reviewers but suffered a misguided review by a prominent scholar who should have known better.[1] Our grandchildren, Robin David Sanders, Jr., was born in 1983 and Alexander Jonathan Sanders in 1986.

---

1. *From Sacred Story to Sacred Text: Canon as Paradigm* (1987; reprinted, Eugene, OR: Wipf & Stock, 2000). Best ignore James Barr's ill-conceived review in which he mistakenly read the book in the light of Brevard S. Childs's work on reading the Bible in a canonical context, with which I largely disagree.

—chapter 20—

South Africa, and the Republican Party

I was invited to spend the winter semester (July to September) of 1989 as visiting research scholar at Stellenbosch University Seminary near Capetown. As already noted I became personally acquainted with Archbishop Desmond Tutu toward the end of our time there. I again was transported back to the American South of my youth because Apartheid was still the policy in South Africa. After the election in early September 1989 the new Prime Minister F. W. De Klerk freed Nelson Mandela from Robbens Island prison and ended Apartheid. But up to that time the Republic of South Africa reflected painfully the South of my youth that I knew so well.

In September of 1995 I was invited to participate in and give a paper at a conference in the University of Heidelberg on the function of heresy in the churches.[1] Christianity has needed heresies in order to have significant dialogue. Whereas Judaism in the historic break from the Jesus movement at the end of the first century had made Torah its core and obedience its raison d'être, Christianity, on the contrary, focused on the biblical story that it claims started in Genesis and culminated in the Christ event. Focusing on the biblical story eventually came to mean acceptance of an orthodox recital of the story so that variance from it became heresy. This tendency culminated in the Grand Inquisition in sixteenth-century Spain and persisted through to the modernist/fundamentalist controversy of the late

1. See Sanders, "Canon as Dialogue," in *Häresien: Religionshermeneutische Studien zur Konstruktion von Norm und Abweichung*, ed. by Irene Pieper et al. (Series Kulte/ Kulturen; Munich: Fink, 2003) 151–67.

nineteenth century. Judaism, on the contrary, declared itself a big enough tent to include numerous interpretations of living a life of Torah—while the dominant Christianity through the ages declared itself the sole custodian of the "true interpretation" of the biblical story and rejected all others as heresy so that heresy became its only way to have real dialogue.

The fact that we had a black president for eight years partially exposed the bigotry of American life. The "solid Democratic South" was horrified by both the Civil Rights Act (1964) and the Voting Rights Act (1965) enacted under President Lyndon Johnson. Then when Arizona Senator Barry Goldwater, campaigning against Johnson in 1964, suggested that Johnson was going too far, followed by President Nixon's "Southern strategy" in the election of 1968, it rapidly became the "solid Republican South." Republican apologists have called this dramatic shift a process, but I was born a Southerner and observed the rapid shift first hand. It was not a process. This was something this former Southerner thought would never happen. But, of course, it did not happen for the right reason, it happened because the Southern bigots in both the Senate and the House realized that they could fight what the Supreme Court and Johnson had done more effectively by becoming Republican. Since its founding by Abraham Lincoln before the Civil War the Republican Party had been the party sponsoring civil rights. On the contrary, the Democratic Party that had ante-dated the War opposed it and even condoned riots against President Lincoln's enactment of the draft.

While this dramatic shift should have horrified the real Republicans in the Party it on the contrary appealed to them as a way to win elections, and it attracted American bigots, like Donald Trump and Texas Sen. Ted Cruz and those who vote for them, to the Party. The Party welcomed bigots like Rush Limbaugh, Sean Hannity, and the Fox News conglomerate to their side. Fox News, an arm of the Republican Party as the president of Ireland recently noted, has sponsored whatever would engender hatred of America's first black president, no matter what it was, even the unconscionable lies they report. It has brought the racism and bigotry of Americans into the open for all to see, and as Glenn Greenwald as noted, the Republican leadership are horrified to see what they have quietly sponsored now out for everyone to see.[2] Conscientious Republicans are scared, but they have brought it on themselves. The Party of Abraham Lincoln and Frederick Douglass has bit the dust, and it still does not want to admit why. Back in 1998 Donald Trump was allegedly quoted in *People Magazine* saying, "If I were to run, I'd run as a Republican. They're the dumbest group of voters in the country. They love anything on Fox News. I could lie and they'd still eat it up." In

---

2. Greenwald, *With Liberty and Justice for Some* (Metropolitan Books, 2011).

addition, most Republicans seem to want to follow Adam Smith's market-centered economic theories almost rigidly without taking into account the crucial, negative factors of human greed and selfishness, the soul mates of racism and bigotry.

The tragic sadness that has emerged from the last some forty years of politicized evangelicalism is that they have almost totally forsaken the Bible they profess to believe in favor of basic American racism and bigotry. Those largely Southern qualities have been the result of their attempt to "evangelize" the rest of the country. And they honestly think they are not only following the Bible but are defending it against modernism and science. They have caused large swaths of citizens to turn against the science evangelicals have fought since the impact of the work of Charles Darwin and the modernist-fundamentalist controversy of the late nineteenth century. They also belittle the human factor in global warming by preaching that Jesus is going to return soon and restore all creation. This encourages folk who prize their individual right of dissension to deny the validity of scientific research and to claim their right as individuals to rely on fire arms to assure their so-called free-will. As Ken Ilgunas remarkably reported after walking the entire length of the Keystone XL Pipeline, "Not one person I encountered said anything even halfway intelligent when denying global warming. . .. They saw themselves as too free-willed and independent to be duped into accepting something that an accomplished and well-trained scientist says is true. . . But it is a false enlightenment to accept only those ideas that align with one's worldview and reject those that don't."[3]

Evangelicals continue to teach "creationism" despite the ludicrous abuse of the Bible evident in the Scopes Trial in Dayton, Tennessee, in 1925. There is a "Creation Museum" in Kentucky, founded by the creationist Ken Ham of the "Answers in Genesis" organization, with the clear intention of defending their misguided, literalist interpretation of the Bible. One supposes that such evangelicals feel the need to defend the one base of authority for their anti-scientific dogmas they have—their mode of reading the Bible. The travesty of the Scopes Trial combined with the farce of Prohibition that was cherished by evangelicals caused evangelicalism for some fifty years to focus on the mission of the saving of individual souls. They believed that if the individual was "saved" or "born-again" he or she would make "the right" decisions in life, and this was the position of evangelicals until the late 1970s. Then in 1979 when it had become clear that it did not have the desired effect, the televangelist, Jerry Falwell, in a famous speech urged evangelicals to get into politics. And they have indeed done so all the while eschewing the discipline of social ethics. The influence of political evangelicalism on the country as a whole can sadly be seen in the fact that Rick Steves in his popular TV series traveling in Europe states that he has to edit out some of the most beautiful, highly cherished, classical art, especially from the Renaissance, found in museums around Europe because of the populist censorship exerted by religious elements in the USA. It is but another example of American hypocrisy when evangelicalism is politicized as it is now.

And speaking of hypocrisy, it lodges easily in colleges, universities, and seminaries that were founded by a specific evangelical group designed to make sure the students are not exposed to critical study of the Bible. I have several times been invited to lecture at such institutions on the Dead Sea Scrolls. Often the department-of-religion faculty would ask me to meet with them alone for a private session about issues of the day unrelated to the Scrolls. We would have a free-for-all discussion as vigorous as any I've been engaged in during meetings of the Society of Biblical Literature or the American Academy of Religion. But invariably the chair of the department would thereafter ask me privately to be sure to avoid any such topic during my lectures but to stick with the discovery and study of the Scrolls only. I understood the concern since to engage in critical study of the Bible with their students or the public would expose them to the charge that they were violating the vows or oath they had to take to be hired in the first place. The anomaly is that the trustees and administration require that those hired on the faculty have doctorates or at least masters degrees from reputable universities but also require them to sign restrictive faith statements prohibiting their teaching what they themselves had been taught.[4] That is patent hypocrisy inflicted on young scholars and their unwitting students by evangelical administrations and their trustees.

---

4. Sanders, "They Dare not Teach What They've Learned," *Biblical Archaeology Review* 36/6 (Nov–Dec 2010) 12.

— chapter 21 —

Bellagio, Fribourg, and Glasgow

In 1985 I received, as already noted, an invitation from the Rockefeller Foundation to take up residence for a month at the Villa Serbelloni in Bellagio northwest of Milan. From the moment Dora and I arrived early in September at the Milano airport, where we were met by a driver from the Villa who secured our bags and drove us through the beautiful Italian northwest countryside up to Bellagio and then up the swerving drive to the Villa entrance, until our departure a month later, we were treated like royalty. We were met at the entrance by the hostess of the Villa and taken to our suite which had been the living quarters of the Principessa who had owned the villa. We had windows looking out over the junction of the two lakes, Como and Lecho. It was little short of decadent, it was posh and beautiful with the gilded faucets and amenities. The first evening all the fellows and spouses who were in residence at the time were feted at a dinner prepared on the veranda overlooking the lake. Our waiter asked which apartment was ours and when I indicated the windows above us he then asked if we knew that President Kennedy had slept there. Quite excited, I blurted out, "Was Jackie with him?" The waiter shook his head and quietly said, "No Sir, It was not Mrs. Kennedy." I said no more, and the waiter went on about his duties. But that night I told Dora whose bed we were sleeping in, including the president's indiscretion.

The purpose of the villa since the Rockefeller Foundation, under Dean Rusk, bought it, with its fifty-five acres of beautiful park and gardens, is to host scholars to work on projects of their choice without interruption or care for upkeep. As another fellow, who had earlier had the experience, said, the experience was "flawless." Unfortunately there was not a person of color in the whole group. We went on from there to have another semester at the

Ecumenical Institute at Tantur north of Bethlehem. Between the two I was able to pull together a book on the concept of canon that was published in 1989.[1]

I was invited by the University of Fribourg in Switzerland to participate in their centenary celebration on August 15, 1990. In conjunction with the invitation I was asked to accept an honorary degree and to conduct a two-week seminar on the Bible as canon prior to the *dies academicus* itself on August 15th. My sponsor was Professor Jean-Dominique Barthélemy, a Dominican and colleague on the UBS research team mentioned above. Because the Holy Office in Rome did not grant the *nihil obstat* to two of the nominees for other honorary degrees also to be granted on the occasion of the centenary celebration I told Dominique that I was uneasy about accepting a degree when others were denied theirs. (There were to have been five scholars from around the world to accept honorary degrees.) The university was founded in 1890 with the support of both the Canton and the Church, so that the Holy Office had the power to withhold approval. The university's response supported by the Canton was to withdraw the granting of honorary degrees on the occasion.

I was very pleased to receive an invitation from Glasgow University to be Alexander Robertson professor of Old Testament for the year 1990–91. I had a wonderful experience and was glad to spend President George H. W. Bush's "Gulf War" in comfortable digs in Faculty Square. It was very instructive to read the various newspapers the Scots were reading about the war. Glasgow was a major center of the eighteenth-century Scottish Enlightenment. It was there that James Watt was first able to harness the power of steam, and where Adam Smith (1723–1790) spent most of his academic life and developed his ideas of a free market expressed in both his well-known books, *Moral Sentiments* and *Wealth of Nations*.[2] I had known that Voltaire, a major figure of the Enlightenment in France of the eighteenth century, had called Scotland the "home of the Enlightenment." One might wonder how and why Scotland produced so many leaders of the Enlightenment, such as David Hume, Adam Smith, and John Locke, but one need not look far beyond the Reformation of John Knox that established the Church of Scotland. Knox's central mission of his Reform was to make sure every Scot could read the Bible for himself. This meant establishing a system of education, quite distinct from the elitist form in England, wherein every Scot could learn to

1. Sanders, *From Sacred Story to Sacred Text: Canon as Paradigm* (1987; reprinted, Eugene, OR: Wipf & Stock, 2000).

2. Adam Smith, *The Theory of Moral Sentiments* (London: Millar, 1759); and Smith, *Inquiry into the Nature and Causes of the Wealth of Nations* (London: Strahan & Cadell, 1776).

read and to study the arts and sciences so that he could think for himself. It made Scotland one of the most highly literate countries at the time in the world. All this, like the Reformation on the continent under Luther and Calvin, was designed, of course, to oppose the Roman Catholic Church's claim to be the sole repository of both heavenly salvation and earthly wisdom. In Scotland, Knox was also battling what was happening "down south" in England, where the mode of education to this day is basically elitist and something like the opposite of the system in Scotland. America copied the Scottish system largely influenced by American Enlightenment figures like Benjamin Franklin and Thomas Jefferson, who were directly responsible for the creation of the Declaration of Independence and the U.S. Constitution.

Most of the "founding fathers" in the USA were Anglican deists who were deeply influenced by the Scottish Enlightenment, and others, many of whom were associated with Glasgow University, the University of Edinburgh, or St. Andrews University. All of the Scots who were part of the Enlightenment were also products of the Church of Scotland, including Adam Smith and Charles Darwin. They thought they were serving God by carefully studying God's creation. But they were also Presbyterian enough to keep in mind the tendency to selfishness and greed of the human soul no matter how influenced by the Enlightenment. Adam Smith was countering governments centered in royalty and monarchy where today the main force in market-based economies are those who climb the market-centered ladder and become as powerful economically and selfish personally as the top-down royal economies of the eighteenth-century. All my teaching life I have stressed with students that the Enlightenment was a gift of God in due season but that it needs the challenges the Bible critically studied offers to keep human selfishness and bigotry in check.[3] I am proud also to hold an honorary doctorate from Glasgow University bestowed earlier in 1975.

3. Richard D. Weis and David M. Carr, eds., *A Gift of God in Due Season: Essays on Scripture and Community in Honor of James A. Sanders* (Sheffield: Sheffield Academic, 1996). Note also Criag A. Evans and Shemaryahu Talmon, eds., *The Quest for Context and Meaning: Studies in Biblical Intertextuality in Honor of James A. Sanders* (Leiden: Brill, 1997).

— chapter 22 —

HEIDELBERG, THE VATICAN, AND RETIREMENT

In 1995 I was invited to join an invited, closed conference at the University of Heidelberg in Germany. The topic of the conference was "heresy" and its functions in the history of religions including Christianity. The conference grew out of an interest of Prof. Jan Assmann, the famous Egyptologist at Heidelberg. The basic conclusion of the conference was that heresies have historically served the need for dialogue, especially in those situations where "heretics" were produced due to intolerance of doctrine of the dominant religion. I was invited not only because of my interest in how the concept of canon arose in Early Judaism and how it spread, but also my work on valorizing the fact that the canon includes in its bounds not only basic monotheizing thrusts but also challenges to how they are understood or misunderstood. The Bible is a dialogical document.

Later in September 1999 I was invited by the Congregatio pro Doctrina Fidei (the Holy Office) to participate in a closed, invited conference on Scripture in the Church. A member of the Vatican conference suggested that the Church always needs to draw up a *regula fidei* through which to read Scripture. I strongly objected arguing that to do so would be to negate Scripture as canon that has always included a rigorous dialogue between Prophetic theology and Wisdom critique. King Solomon, it is claimed in 1 Kings, asked not for long life, honor, or riches but for Wisdom to the benefit of the people he governed (1 Kings 3:5–14); but it also noted that Solomon "spoke of trees, from the cedar that is in Lebanon to the hyssop that grows out of the wall, beasts, birds, reptiles, and fish." Like Aristotle, in contrast to Plato, he looked down at God's creation and not up at forms in the heavens. A *regula fidei* would in effect eliminate the force of canon in Christian history that has given rise to "sects" and "denominations" to challenge various interpretations of it.[1] There were no blacks or others of color at either conference.

I was formally retired from the Claremont School of Theology (CST) and the Claremont Graduate University in May 1997. The retirement dinner was a splendid occasion where a number of former students returned to share their experiences working on their doctorates and helping expand the role and services of the Ancient Biblical Manuscript Center in biblical scholarship around the world. Earlier that spring I had been invited to spend the first year of retirement as visiting professor back at Union Theological Seminary and Columbia University. Other invitations for teaching in retirement came from Yale University Divinity School (YDS) in New Haven and Jewish Theological Seminary (JTS) in New York. In fact, I was invited several times thereafter to teach courses at JTS, experiences I truly cherish. Back in Southern California I taught courses at Shepherd University in Korea-town in Los Angeles over several years. Then beginning in 2005 I became professor of biblical studies for the Episcopal Theological Seminary in Claremont (Bloy House) where I continue to teach up to this writing. In fact at this point I have completed 62 years of teaching and have no plans as yet to cease or desist. I continue to serve on a couple of editorial boards for journals in my field and am occasionally asked by colleagues to read manuscripts they have written before they submit them to publishers. One of these has been the work of Weston Fields, executive director of the Dead Sea Scrolls Foundation, of which I am a member of its board of directors since its inception in 1991.[2] While Union Seminary in New York and the Claremont School of Theology have a good percentage of blacks or others of color, both on the faculty and in the student body, Yale Divinity School until recently had few or no professors of color of any sort. Even when I taught at YDS in 1998 there were no professors of color among the celebratory ranks of photos of faculty in the Commons area.

One of the reasons I feel compelled to continue to teach future leaders of the churches is that racism and bigotry continue to flourish in the American experience. Committing genocide against native Americans and dehumanizing blacks through slavery and subsequent Jim Crowism have been the salient marks of American democracy since its very beginning.[3] After

1. See Sanders, "God's Work in the Secular World," *Biblical Theology Bulletin* 37 (2004) 145–52.

2. See Weston W. Fields, *The Dead Sea Scrolls: A Short History* (Leiden: Brill, 2006); and Fields, *The Dead Sea Scrolls: A Full History*, vol. 1 (Leiden: Brill, 2009).

3. See the gripping account of "the shocking horrors of slavery" practiced in

the Supreme Court issued its judgments against Apartheid in education in the country, especially in the South, a group of Southern Senators and Representatives (in fact, most of them) issued a "Declaration of Constitutional Principles"—better known as "The Southern Manifesto." It was a mark of defiance of the Constitution in the name of it; Southern politicians are especially capable of twisting the text of the Constitution in order to mask American bigotry of its many shapes and sizes.[4] One can see the same kind of abuse of a document in the multiple efforts of white evangelicals to hide bigotry behind a few biblical passages. As Father Daniel Berrigan noted, they follow "a scrap-book Bible" of their own making. They then claim that their superimposed doctrine of biblical inerrancy means that what they say is supported by the entire Bible. They abused the Bible to support slavery and then Apartheid. Failing at that they abuse the Bible to support bigotry against lesbians, gays, bisexuals, and transgender folk. They seem to need to have some group to debase. Trying undoubtedly to appear reasonable an evangelical recently assured me that homosexuality is a pathology. My response is that that attitude itself is the pathology.

The politicized evangelical movement has distorted its origins in the Second Great Awakening of the nineteenth century to the point of becoming a secular, political force in the country reviving the farces of Prohibition and the Scopes Trial. They still claim that homosexuality is a choice that a gay or lesbian makes. Why? In order to defend the one authority they have left: their particular interpretation of the Bible. They defend American biases by citing the Bible which was written and shaped in the Iron-Age to Hellenistic cultural metaphors and idioms of the times in which it was written. They easily ignore the Bible when it suits them, such as Our Lord's condemnation of divorce, but cite select verses out of context in order to condemn "others." It should be no surprise that a majority of white evangelicals support Donald Trump. Why? Because white evangelicalism has become a political movement and Trump amply supports their xenophobia and bigotry.

Those same evangelicals support the State of Israel without regard to justice or the welfare of the Christian and Muslim inhabitants, the Palestinians. They dehumanize Palestinians because they get in the way of the evangelical schema of what they believe will be the "return of the Christ" promised, in their view, to come after the re-establishment of "Israel." Since their eschatological hermeneutic in reading certain verses of the Bible requires the re-establishment of a Jewish state before they believe Christ will

America in Colson Whitehead, *Underground Railroad: A Novel* (New York: Doubleday, 2016).

4. See the op-ed article by Justin Driver, "The Southern Manifesto," *Los Angeles Times*, March 11, 2016.

return they support Zionism without question without regard to the humanity of and justice for the Palestinians. They totally dismiss concern for social ethics and particularly the rights of the Palestinians in their eagerness to hail the Return of Christ—as they have worked it out in their particular reading of the biblical text. And while they openly support the State of Israel now, they claim that Jews will all become Christian when Christ returns. Zionists who accept the evangelical schema now will regret it sooner than later.

Erich Mendelsohn, the famous architect who fled to Palestine in 1934, published a pamphlet suggesting that "Zionism must not only accommodate but unite with the population already present in Palestine." He called on Jews to become a cell of "a future Semitic commonwealth modeled on the medieval golden age of Arab rule when Jews and Arabs together acted as torch bearers of world enlightenment."[5] But alas, that was almost ninety years ago when Judaism was not yet identified with politicized Zionism and seems like a distant dream of the essential goodness of humanity essentially destroyed by the Holocaust and understandably but sadly the deep-seated but understandable suspicion by Jews today of the rest of humanity.

I am loath to conclude this memoir on such a note. I am deeply proud of my doctorate from the Hebrew Union College and deeply grateful for my two saving experiences. At 88 years of age I know that the time left to sing the praises of the One God of us all, and to live like it in this short human journey, is limited now to whatever time left I have to render thanks that I have been called to witness to the Oneness and Integrity of the One God of us All. Rendering thanks is not limited to words but is best expressed in living out one's belief that we on this tiny speck of dust we call Earth are all creatures and children of the same God, no matter the names or metaphors for or stories about God different cultures use.[6]

5. Quoted from the *Los Angeles Times*, 24 April 2016.
6. Note the appendix to *The Monotheizing Process*, 62–82: "Credo in Unum Deum."

— Appendix —

THE BETRAYAL OF EVANGELICALISM[1]

I was born and raised in Memphis, Tennessee, and was "saved" at a young age in a tent revival meeting that eventually became the First Assembly of God Church, before Elvis Presley had his experience in the same church at a different location, and well before its expansion nationwide.

I still cherish the experience I had that night kneeling in the sawdust leaning on the two-by-four make-shift pew in front of me where I lay my head and raised my hand. It was in the depths of the Great Depression and even as a child I sensed its importance to those who attended largely because many didn't know when the next payday might be. My older sister had taken me partly as a shield for a date she had that night though she herself claimed to live at times in a state of grace because of that little church.

At the same time, I enjoyed school and academic endeavor generally and was discovering the wonders of reading the literature of other cultures and of learning the insights of science into God's amazing creation. Learning became a passion fired by curiosity about this wondrous world so that there developed a pitched battle inside me between my head and my heart—that was until I had a second "saving" experience in college when I learned it didn't have to be that way but that I could worship God as an integrated, whole person.[2] Later in the 1960s and 1970s while I was a professor at the Union Theological Seminary in New York City, after I had unrolled and published the large Dead Sea Scroll of Psalms, and not long before I had

---

1. This essay first appeared in *Bulletin of the Colgate Rochester Crozer Divinity School* (Summer 2012) 8-13, 18-22.

2. Sanders, *God Has a Story Too* (1979; reprinted, Eugene, OR: Wipf & Stock, 2000) ix–xi.

been elected President of the International Society of Biblical Literature, I became a "member under watch-care" (associate member) in the Concord Baptist Church of Christ in Bedford-Stuyvesant (in Brooklyn, New York) where Gardner Taylor was pastor. I was distressed by the debates in the white churches at the time about whether they should focus on preaching the Gospel or addressing social issues. The black congregation of Concord Church did both; each effort fed the other without reference to politics.

Despite my warm appreciation for the evangelical experience, I have come deeply to regret the politicization of the white evangelical movement that has taken place since the late 1970s.

In the light of the current political chasm that has developed in the country, it is time to look at some of the current characteristics of evangelicalism that are deeply disturbing and bode ill for the nation.

The So-called "Moral Majority"

In 1979 Rev. Jerry Falwell launched what he called The Moral Majority movement. His target was ostensibly the apparent excesses in the late 1960s and early 1970s of change in the moral culture of the country. His announced target was the apparent loosening of personal morals, especially among young people: the use of drugs, the practice of free sex and the increasing acceptance of abortion and homosexuality in mainstream America. These seemed to have increased dramatically during the protests at the time against the Vietnam War and against racism in America. Falwell struck a chord among some people in the country who viewed themselves as hard-working, upstanding adherents of "old family values." The struggle was soon called "culture wars," struggles to resist what were viewed as efforts to destroy the moral fabric of society, the very sinews of what held society and the tacit social contract intact. It launched the "New Religious Right."

Unspoken, but at the base of the objections, were the disturbing (to some) advances that had been made during the 1960s in civil rights and civil liberties in the country giving "others" (blacks, browns, recent immigrants) the same right to vote and to access evenhanded justice as though they were "real" citizens. Just as disturbing to many were the findings of science that went counter to their beliefs.[3] Falwell, in an oft-quoted speech in 1979, said that evangelicals in the country should change their attitude toward a longstanding limit imposed on themselves and their leaders (since

---

3. Neal Gabler, "Politics as Religion in America: Religion Has Been Converted into a Religious Belief and Now Compromise Doesn't Have a Prayer," *Los Angeles Times*, 2 Oct. 2009, Opinion page.

Prohibition) to limit their "Christian" mission to the individual's salvation and personal morals in American life. Evangelical Christianity since the farce of the Scopes Trial and the disaster of Prohibition had largely limited its energies to seeking the salvation of individual souls, who once "saved," it was thought, make "right" decisions. Falwell apparently felt that the old view was not working well from his viewpoint and that American Christians needed to be told what right decisions were. Falwell's speech rang a clarion bell among many "middle-America" Christians who watched the anti-war and anti-racism demonstrations on television—what they called "riots"—with great unease, even embarrassment, that these were occurring in "their" country. Many of them had felt that while America had problems they should be addressed by elected officials who had access to the information others did not and who knew best about such matters. The country, as well as their religion, was being attacked from within, many felt, and enough was enough.

The reaction was especially pronounced in the so-called Bible Belt, largely in the old South, where it was deeply felt that President Lyndon Johnson and the Democrats had gone too far with their civil rights and civil liberties legislation in the mid-1960s and that something should be done about it before it ruined the country they knew and loved. Presidential candidate Barry Goldwater in 1964 campaigned in part against Johnson's civil rights laws and Senator Strom Thurmond of South Carolina defected from the Democratic Party to the Republican—the first crack in the old Democratic "solid South," as it was called. President Johnson at the time told Bill Moyer, a confidant and fellow former Texan, that because of the advances made, the Democratic Party had lost the solid Democratic South. More public was candidate Richard Nixon's "Southern strategy" in his 1968 campaign against the Democrat Hubert Humphrey. Nixon, the "right-wing progressive" Republican candidate indicated clearly during the campaign, especially to his former colleagues in the United States Congress, the vast majority of them Southern Democrats, that he fully intended to modify some of the purported "excesses" of the laws Johnson had sponsored, and an increasing number defected at that time, including Senator Jesse Helms of North Carolina and numerous members of the House of Representatives.

Humphrey, on the contrary, to counter the bad publicity he had accrued being Johnson's "happy warrior" in the steady increase of America's involvement in the Vietnam War, touted the legislation he and Johnson had successfully steered through Congress in the wake of John F. Kennedy's assassination and subsequent populist martyrdom. Nixon's strategy worked and Humphrey's did not. The disgruntled "heartland majority" who had been offended by the demonstrations against the war (that they felt were really against their America), voted in droves for Nixon while those who would normally have supported Humphrey stayed away because of his support of the war. Nixon's efforts during his first term to curb some aspects of the civil rights laws and at the same time advance social legislation that was still needed, such as extensions of Johnson's Medicare legislation, and other efforts that would today be condemned by some as socialist, were a winning combination at the time and Nixon was handily re-elected in 1972, defeating the peace candidate, George McGovern.

Nixon's personal insecurities, however, ultimately undid him in the Watergate Affair that revealed a Republican break-in of the Democratic headquarters in Washington—authorized by the Nixon White House—in a flawed attempt to win the election against McGovern. Nixon since his loss to Kennedy in the presidential election of 1960 and his loss of the gubernatorial race in California to Pat Brown in 1962, had developed an inferiority complex that fed his illegal acts in the Watergate break-in. By August 1974 Nixon's own personal complicity in the crime was confirmed by the Supreme Court, and he was forced to resign the presidency soon after. This web of perfidy is often cited as Nixon's greatest flaw, but arguably it was not. The greater ill he committed against the country was not in the Watergate Affair but in his "Southern strategy," by which he set the country back to a degree that is still being played out at the beginning of the twenty-first century. Nixon, following Goldwater's earlier lead, in effect converted the Republican Party, that had since Abraham Lincoln been the party of civil rights, into a Southern bastion of reactionary politics. With or without Nixon, the South that had lost the Civil War conquered the Republican Party and through a regional form of Christianity began to evangelize the rest of the country. It has been noted that "evangelical Christianity has driven a wedge between Southern and Northern interests. It intruded into the political process so that there was no middle ground. There was only good and evil . . ."[4]

Scripture and Authority

Through the influence of the Enlightenment, mainstream Christianity came to view the Holy Spirit as the liberator from the cultural traps and trappings of the ancient eastern Mediterranean cultures in which the Bible was formed and shaped. It was seen as the guide of the faithful into accepting the advances in the developing disciplines of science. Reducing the base of

---

4. David Goldfield, *America Aflame: How the Civil War Created a Nation* (New York: Bloomsbury, 2011).

authority to Scripture alone has meant that some evangelicals have felt it necessary to attack any serious effort that would challenge their interpretations of Scripture, including science. Since Charles Darwin's work in the mid-nineteenth century, the greatest challenge has seemed to come from science. Since the Second Great Awakening in the early nineteenth century evangelicals have tried to assert the Bible's authority even in understanding how the world and its denizens were formed, thus in effect denigrating the Bible's real worth and value. But it is quite understandable that if you have narrowed your range of authority to one base, then you have to attack whatever seems to challenge it. Darwin, like Galileo before him, personally believed that his work in science was a pious endeavor exploring the wonders of God's creation and hence was astounded at the opposition from some Christians. The evangelicals' denunciation of Darwin's work has extended to their renunciation of scientific findings that point to human causes of global warming, and it often takes the form of ad hominem arguments accusing the scientists of personal bias or conspiracy. The last decades of such pseudo-arguments have caused countless young people to turn away from science. If it weren't for the number of brilliant immigrants who came to the United States and studied science, the country would lose its ranking in scientific discovery.

This concerned Albert Einstein so much that he pled fervently for a change in attitude, saying that "we have to remind our kids that a math equation formula is just a brush stroke the good Lord uses to paint one of the wonders of nature, and we should look at it as being as beautiful as art or literature or music."[5]

This anti-science posture is a part of the traditional anti-intellectual strain in some branches of Protestantism since the Reformation when there were only Catholic-based universities in Europe that some Protestants at the time refused to attend. It continued to serve well during the westward expansion of this country since at first there were often no schools at all on the frontiers and only much later colleges and schools of higher education. To this day most independent community-type megachurches do not require theological education or intellectual rigor. This serves the anti-environmentalist stance by casting doubt on scientific reports that contradict their beliefs. Focus on the imminent Rapture of believers and the Second Coming further diminishes any urgency about dangers to the environment. Jesus will return and make everything all right again so that they don't have to be concerned. The fact that every prediction of the arrival of the end of the

5. Walter Isaacson, *Einstein: His Life and Universe* (New York: Simon & Schuster, 2007).

world based on "Bible prophecy" has been proved wrong over the centuries has in no way deterred further efforts to make eschatological calculations.[6]

It also includes what some evangelicals refer to as a "Biblical world view," meaning, one would suppose, that the image of the universe in the Bible of a flat three-storied structure, heaven, earth and hell, is the correct one. Well, no, we are told, not exactly "flat." What they mean, we are told, is that though the earth is a sphere (anyone can see that from an airplane, and astronauts have sent pictures back of how it is) there is still a heaven and hell somewhere in God's "good space." But "somewhere" is not what the Bible offers, it assumes as all the Ancient Near East assumed, that the earth was flat in a three-tiered world. Defense of the Biblical account of the flood has constantly been modified in a like manner by admitting that there were many flood stories like that described in the Bible but the others (against all evidence to the contrary) must have borrowed from the Bible—thus accepting what cannot be avoided from archaeology and philology but hanging on for dear life to what they can of their view of the "authority" of the Biblical account.

Some older evangelical groups have vested so much authority in their interpretation of Scripture alone that they have founded their own free-standing seminaries to shield future pastors and leaders from serious challenges to it. The same seminaries almost invariably require professors to sign binding statements of faith centering in their view of the authority of Scripture. One of the ironies of the current situation is that they also require their professors to have solid Ph.D. degrees from reputable institutions. The principal irony is that the faculty, well educated in critical understandings of Scripture and tradition, is caught in a vise between the conservative trustees of such institutions, who raise the funds to run the school, and the conservative students s/he teaches, many of whom come from the homes of trustees and like-minded supporters. I have personally experienced and seen the vise they are in because I have been invited to lecture on the Dead Sea Scrolls in several of those institutions and have talked privately with the faculties in them and heard their stories first-hand. Alone, in camera, we had vigorous critical-historical discussions about the Bible, but I was invariably requested that in class and public lectures on campus I lecture only about the Scrolls and not get into the kinds of critical issues we had just openly discussed behind closed doors.

6. Jonathan Kirsch, *A History of the End of the World* (San Francisco: HarperSan-Francisco, 2006).

The South's Victory

The sum of Goldwater and Nixon's actions, despite the ignominious defeat of the Confederacy in the Civil War, was in effect to aid and abet the South's "rise again" by placing reactionary Southerners in responsible party and government positions and to aid the effort on the part of the Southern Baptist Convention and Southern-types of evangelical Christianity to "evangelize" former slave-free states as well as the South to their way of thinking. The Southern Baptist Convention during its annual convention of 1975 was taken over by a group from Texas led by laymen (with little or no theological education) who caused the Convention and a number of its agencies to turn away from its earlier progressive views to "the fundamentals," as they viewed them, of the Christian faith. Each Baptist congregation is autonomous, but the Convention holds considerable power over its agencies and committees. With religious fervor the fundamentalist-leaning evangelicals have in the name of their view of Christianity converted large swaths of the "heartland" of the country to Southern ways of religious and political thinking.

The Southern Baptist Convention in the 1980s officially instigated a mission movement to "evangelize" the rest of the country. It has been successful to the point of affecting what has been called the "southernization of American politics."[7] The newly figured Convention quickly moved to control the denomination's seminaries. As a result I was personally no longer invited to lecture at Southern Baptist seminaries. Since the takeover I have had invitations from progressive Southern Baptist pastors to address their small groups seeking encouragement to continue their ministries even while they are denounced and shunned by fellow pastors in the local conventions. The personal stories I have heard from such well-educated pastors about the treatment to which they are subjected is very disheartening.

The election in 1982 of Ronald Reagan, a movie actor from California who had converted from being a labor-oriented leader of the Screen Actors Guild to become its Republican governor, brought the country to another low point with lies about the Iran-Contra Affair. Reagan, knowing little or nothing of religion, was far more to the liking of the reactionaries, and he was personally affable and very likeable. It was easy to forgive and forget, that had not been the case with Nixon. He turned to Falwell and other evangelicals as consultants on some of the country's most important political matters. For seasoned theologians in the country and the world, Reagan's consulting Falwell and calling him "a theologian" was a travesty and became for some a symbol of his presidency. Reagan drew on the old Republican

7. David Bromwich, "The Rebel Germ," *New York Review of Books* 57 (25 Nov. 2010) 18.

desire to limit the power of the federal government and went so far as to call government "the problem and not the solution" to the country's ills. Reagan was the "savior" that had been sought to oppose Johnson's enactment of the civil rights, voting rights and health-care legislation in the 1960s. Reagan's antigovernment stance has recently been taken to mean opposition to much of Johnson's legislation that advanced those rights, including Medicare and any other effort by the government for the common good of the country.

The politicization of the religious right in the country abetted by Reagan, and G.W. Bush (not his New England Republican father) brought about a consolidation of opposition to any further enactment in the Congress of legislation to bring the country into closer adherence to the principles of its Constitution. One of the ironies of the present situation is the claim of the religious right to being strict constructionists of the principles of the Constitution. This is far from the truth of the matter.[8] The Constitution mandates the separation of church and state whereas evangelicals, professing belief in both the Bible and the Constitution, have attempted a sort of amalgam of the two doing great harm to the public's understanding of both. In contradistinction to the Constitution, the Bible tells the story of a theocracy whose God was King no matter who His representatives on Earth charged with divulging and executing His will, whether patriarchs, "judges," prophets, kings or priests.[9] Any effort to impose Biblical legal principles upon those of the new republic was prohibited as inherently opposed to the principles clearly laid out in the Declaration of Independence and the Constitution.[10] The same religious leaders fervently support only secular-type governments in Arab lands failing to see the analogy to their own efforts.

Deists and Theists

The Declaration and the Constitution were drawn up and "framed" by eighteenth-century Enlightenment deists, not by Christian theists as is often claimed by the Religious Right. The deists were profoundly influenced by the writings of David Hume and John Locke. In fact, it has been noted that some of the most majestic phrases employed in the Declaration were borrowed whole-cloth out of the work of John Locke. Evangelical leaders have claimed that the framers believed in God. (One current candidate for

8. David L. Holmes, *The Faith of the Founding Fathers* (Oxford: Oxford University Press, 2006).

9. Martin Buber, *Kingship of God* (New York: Harper & Row, 1967).

10. Jon Meacham, *American Gospel: God, The Founding Fathers and the Making of a Nation* (New York: Random House, 2006).

president has claimed that the founders did not have slaves, but that has been easily dismissed as sheer ignorance.) Their view of God was a deistic God, not the Christian theistic God, and that is a vital distinction that most Americans do not appreciate. The theist's view of God may indeed be called a personal deity, but not a deist's view of God that was distant and ineffable, a God of nature. As a movement, the eighteenth-century Enlightenment was viewed by many deists as countering the theistic views of most forms of Christianity, especially the Trinitarian view of God. In fact, later in the nineteenth century the deist Ralph Waldo Emerson stated his belief that Christians in this country would eventually all profess a Unitarian view of God, not a Christian theistic view.

Thomas Jefferson, responsible for much of the writing of the founding documents, was a deist who produced an edition of the New Testament that totally eliminated the miracles and most passages exhibiting theistic views. In fact, one would think that if justices believe that the Constitution is a "dead document," supposedly meaning that it should be interpreted with its original meanings, they would decide a number of cases differently based on the way it has recently been interpreted. The Constitution is thus inherently in opposition to much of the Bible's assumptions of Israel and the Christian Church as theocratic. To wrap oneself in the flag, as some politicians try to do, should mean that they are opposed to any particularly religious view of the Constitution, indeed of the Republic it established on these shores. Those who insist on erecting crosses and crèches on public land, and the addition of "In God We Trust" to coinage actually cheapen such phrases, as well as cross and crèche, into general cultural icons of religious fervor and weaken the Christian meaning of such symbols.

The question arises as to how the generation that framed the Declaration and the Constitution was followed by generations of evangelical Christians.[11] Or, put another way, how did the colonies from Virginia all the way south to Georgia turn from being states that were mostly Anglican to being largely evangelical. The answer lies in the immigrant expansion west of the Alleghenies and into the Appalachians south, and also beyond the Ohio and Mississippi rivers. The brave new immigrants who ventured south and west after the east coast British colonies became the United States were not Anglican but largely Scotch-Irish, neo-Puritan, evangelical Christians. McGuffey's Reader became the stock textbook of most public schools in the mid- to late-nineteenth century and is still in use, largely in home-school

---

11. William Strauss and Neil Howe, *Generations: The History of America's Future, 1584 to 2069* (New York: Morrow, 1991) 97–110, et passim.

efforts.[12] It represents the Puritans of Plymouth Rock and Anglo-Saxons as the original Americans, instead of the wide variety of immigrants that originally made up the American ethnos, not only British rejected subjects but Dutch, French, and Spanish explorers, not to mention Native Americans whom we dispossessed and AfroAmericans whom we forced to migrate here, and many others since who continued and continue to enrich the country. The latest wave is usually viewed with great suspicion, whether legal or illegal, particularly those of other than North European origin. As Karl Shapiro has aptly said, "The European Jew was always a visitor . . . But in America everybody is a visitor."[13]

Very different from the First Great Awakening of the eighteenth century, which was heavily influenced by the Enlightenment, the so-called Second Awakening beginning in the early nineteenth century and continuing through to the modernist/fundamentalist controversy ending in the first quarter of the twentieth century, was evangelical, pentacostal, revivalist and Bible-oriented.[14] The eighteenth century is aptly called the Age of Reason, the century of the Enlightenment, while the nineteenth is instead called the Romantic Age when reason and intellect gave way to a surge of quite different thinking in which stamina for life on the frontier and valor and honor in battle became dominant themes.

The extreme of this was in the recent evangelical support of G. W. Bush's Iraq War with the specious argument that the Iraqis would get to hear "the message of Jesus Christ." The opposite has occurred and Christians with deep roots throughout the Near East are now in grave danger.

The invasions have provoked extreme Islamisists in those lands to attack and persecute the Christians already there, but this probably won't deter such an argument in future. There has been a tendency as well for some Christians to speak of "our God" over against "their God" unaware apparently that to say such things is classic henotheism, that is, belief in one God per tribe, people, or religion and not monotheism that holds that there is but One God of All. Jesus was the ultimate monotheizer when he argued that God was the God of Romans as well as of Jews and that his followers should love their enemies and forgive those who hate them (Matthew 5:44).

In the nineteenth century the change suited the country well in its American-Zionist quest for manifest destiny of God's "true Israel on these shores," thereby establishing "empire." Orientation toward Britain and

12. William Holmes McGuffey, *The Eclectic First Reader for Children with Pictures*, 1st ed. (Cincinnati: Truman & Smith, 1841).

13. Karl Shapiro, *In Defense of Ignorance* (New York: Vintage, 1965).

14. Garry Wills, *Head and Heart: American Christianities* (New York: Penguin, 2007), 121–350.

Europe waned considerably in the wake of the War of 1812, and attention turned to conquering the vast territory west to the Pacific Ocean. American Zionism, or belief in American exceptionalism as God's True Zion, developed during the nineteenth century beyond its beginnings with the Calvinist ideology of the Puritans and became a dominant theme in most of the evangelical sects of the period: America was God's true Israel and divinely blessed "o'er amber waves of grain . . . from sea to shining sea." Roman Catholics were deeply opposed to the Zionist ideology and refused to join in the "public education" movement that they saw as dominated by it and as expressed in McGuffey's Reader. They thus established Catholic parochial schools wherever they settled in the country. Their spiritual allegiance was as much to Rome as to America.

The neo-Puritan, evangelical strain in the American character reached something of a climax in the enactment of Prohibition, its most successful penetration into the Constitution with the eighteenth amendment to it in 1920. The neo-Puritan experiment exposed America's hypocritical trait in the closing of saloons but the overwhelming success in their place of "blind-pigs" and "speakeasies." The government, many of whose leaders were either against Prohibition or hypocrites publicly supporting it but privately violating it with regularity, simply refused to allot the money needed to enforce the law and it failed until it was repealed in 1933, happily endorsed by the new president, Franklin Roosevelt, an Episcopalian. Episcopalians, like Jews, Catholics and most Lutherans never supported Prohibition, even opposed it.

The Southern Mind and Culture

Evangelical Christianity succeeded also in outlawing the teaching of evolution in many areas, mostly in the South. During the middle of Prohibition, in 1925, a high-school teacher in Dayton, Tennessee, was indicted for teaching it. Most well educated teachers—even in the South—taught evolution, but John Scopes became the scapegoat and was tried in one of the most famous public trials in the history of the country. William Jennings Bryan, an evangelical lawyer, argued for the State of Tennessee and Clarence Darrow for the defense. Scopes was convicted and fined $100. But Bryan and Darrow both felt that the real debate had yet to take place and the judge allowed them to hold it after the trial was over in the shade on the lawn of the courthouse where the summer heat had become oppressive. The debate attracted crowds not only in the area but drew a vast national audience by being one of the first nation-wide broadcasts of a newly formed national radio network. When the debate was over, polls were taken in the North and in the South with opposite results. The North voted decisively in favor of Darrow's arguments while most of the South felt that Bryant had won the debate. Here was a clear-cut sampling of the difference in mentality, even culture, at the time between the old Confederacy and the Northern States. The South, in which I was born and raised, was marked by emotionalism and militarism. Mark Twain noted that after the Civil War, Northerners sometimes referred to the war in passing, but Southerners invariably re-ferred to it in very personal terms with continued hatred of the dreaded Yankees who had forced them to their knees to change their lives so drasti-cally.[15] A common expression in my youth was, "I was a grown man before I learned that 'damned-yankee' was two words."

Southern evangelicals have recently launched a serious mission to convert the rest of the country to their political views, and the Republican Party has become a vehicle for doing so. More recently it has been manifest in the evangelical resistance to granting equal Constitutional rights to gays and lesbians and to once again limiting the rights of women, in essence putting their view and interpretation of the Bible above the mandates of the Constitution.

Mainstream Christian denominations in the country, and some evan-gelicals like Jim Wallis and his magazine *Sojourners*, oppose the politicized evangelical understanding of the Bible and continue to offer the country a sane, rational form of evangelicalism based on historical-critical readings of it. They firmly believe that the Holy Spirit is God's way of leading Christians in modern times forward beyond the ancient cultural mores in which the Bible was written to celebrate the advances of science in all its fields as the work of God every bit as much as the Bible was in the Ancient Near Eastern and Greco-Roman cultures through which it was expressed and written.

Thus when Southern-style evangelical Christianity became politicized at the beginning of the last quarter of the twentieth century, the kind of mentality that ushered in Prohibition and forbade the teaching of the sci-ence of evolution at the beginning of the century gained a resurgence of influence that eventually became a major element again of the Republican Party at the beginning of the twenty-first century. It reached a sort of zenith in the presidency of G. W. Bush, an avowed evangelical who publicly pro-fessed to read the Bible every day for inspiration in governing the country. One wonders how often he read and pondered the Constitution.

And, of course, he read the Bible in the highly personal, non-historical, un-critical mode typical of the evangelical. Since William Jennings Bryan

15. Mark Twain, *Life on the Mississippi* (New York: Penguin, 1991), 275–82.

had failed in his three bids for the presidency, Bush became the first sitting president in such a mold to govern the country, a clear gain by evangelicalism to missionize the whole country. The mission of evangelicals to seek the conversion of individuals, which marked their solid contribution to American culture between the Scopes Trial and the "Moral Majority" movement, got lost in their desire to influence the country instead by strengthening their hold on the Republican Party, much to the detriment of the party and to the country as a whole.

Traits of Current Evangelicalism

As a movement, evangelicalism:

— promotes rank individualism with a limited sense of responsibility for the common good, yet attempts to influence legislation with views of individual morality imposed upon the whole nation. It is the result of the far Western climax of the Hellenizing process (following the Renaissance) that yielded the positive results of democracy and of human and civil rights yet opposes support of government for the common good and opposes efforts to curb inhumanity and injustice;

— seeks to limit the rights of individual gays, women and others to suit their views of individual morality through the political process;

— lacks a concept of "church." Salvation, according to evangelicalism, is in the individual's "acceptance of the Lord Jesus Christ as personal savior," with little sense of church as the people of God or as the locus of salvation, but rather as local congregations of "saved" individuals;

— claims that personhood begins at conception, an attempt to abolish abortions and limit the rights of women;

— arrogates the term "Christian" to their views alone as though Orthodox, Catholic and main-line Protestants are not;

— limits concept of Holy Spirit. Whereas liberals view the work of the Holy Spirit as leading Christianity on out beyond the ancient cultural trappings of the Bible, evangelical/fundamentalists limit the work of the Holy Spirit to inspiration of the individual preacher and believer;

— rejects historical/critical readings of the Bible in order to read the Bible through modern individualist culture and thought;

— uses the Bible to sanction bias in the same manner it was used to support slavery;

— claims that "social ethics is the work of the Devil," ignoring vast portions of the Prophets, the Gospels and Paul's Epistles;

— supports candidates who, when elected to legislatures and Congress, refuse to compromise on deciding issues;

— resists "compromise as the art of politics," the principle of effective legislation since ancient Greece, embodied in the wisdom of modern sages like Walter Rauschenbusch and Reinhold Niebuhr, carrying over from Sunday School admonitions as youth not to compromise into community and government issues;

— confuses principle with bias, making many evangelical churches a refuge to retain cultural prejudices unchallenged;

— absorbs churches, like Pentecostals and the Assembly of God churches, into evangelical bibliolatry that originally focused on the Holy Spirit and opposed the fundamentalist idolatry of Scripture;

— ignores large portions of the Bible to focus on compatible passages that support "prophecy" of the end-time;

— focuses on homosexuality as the "sin of the age," thus providing a smokescreen that masks bigotry, selfishness and greed, and forcing LGBT Christians to live in the closet, thus living lies;

— blames homosexuality on the individual's choice though science has shown this is not so, causing suicides among youth because they know inside themselves that if truthful they will be rejected and forfeit the love and acceptance of parents, family and peers;

— blames homosexuals' wish to marry as the cause of the demise of marriage whereas the high rate of divorce in the country is the real cause of the decline of respect for marriage vows, and a shield of the fact that over 52% of marriages in the Bible Belt end in divorce. Jesus's condemnation of divorce (Luke 16:18; Matthew 5:32) and silence about homosexuality is conveniently ignored, like many of the Bible's explicit commandments;

— focuses on eschatology to the detriment of the challenge of the Prophetic and Gospel messages against idolatry, bigotry, and greed;

— focuses on the Rapture, thereby sanctioning abandonment of responsibility for the earth and for fellow humans, and for the damage humans are doing to the earth and its 30 trillion dollar annual endowment, steadily destroying the value that nature provides for renewal of air, soil and water supplies;

— denigrates "science" when its work and results seem to challenge their reading of the Bible, despite hypocritically enjoying its many benefits and advantages;

— denigrates government out of fear of the sort China has, even to the point of vilifying the social advantages of government-run health care and similar advantages the rest of first-world industrial nations enjoy;

— denigrates learning from other cultures and nations no matter how valuable for us because of a belief in American exceptionalism.

Conclusion

As the nation moves further into the second decade of the twenty-first century, the influence of politicized evangelicalism in the country is at its highest point since the passage of Prohibition. The outcome of the national elections has revealed how great the divide is and will probably indicate how influential politicized evangelicalism has become over the last thirty years. I personally continue to be deeply appreciative of the experiences I had as a youth in the evangelical movement during the mid-twentieth century, but I am greatly disturbed at how politicized to the radical right it has become— to its own detriment, to that of the country generally and especially to the detriment of the American political process.

·Post-Scriptum·

DORA GEIL CARGILLE SANDERS
1928–2016

My precious wife and best friend, born 5 March 1928, in Newark, New Jersey, died Sunday evening, 12 June 2016, of complications of dementia just as I was completing the above manuscript.

The dementia had become evident a few years earlier and gradually affected her bodily functions during the last two years until death when it came was a blessing. At death her face went from distress and pain to a form of beauty that nearly overwhelmed me. I fell in love all over again and gently kissed her forehead, eyes, nose, and lips in an effort to convey to her parting spirit my renewed devotion expressed in our marriage vows taken on 30 June 1951 in the Temple Protestant on Rue Madame in the Sixième Arrondissement of Paris near the beautiful Church of Saint Sulpice where we often had gone to hear the transporting music of Marcel Dupré at its famous organ.

We would have celebrated our sixty-fifth anniversary this year. Dora was a violinist, pianist, organist, modern dancer, photographer for dance, massage therapist for dancers, motorcyclist, skier, and accomplished swimmer. She participated in the American Dance Festival every summer from 1949 to 2004. Before she could get a license to drive she flew planes for the Civil Air Patrol along the New Jersey coast during World War II (beginning at age 16) looking for German U-boats. She was, in sum, a remarkable woman who devoted her eighty-eight years to making others feel good about themselves. She never called attention to herself. She didn't need to.

INDEX

Acadia University, 68, 72
Albina, Najib (photographer), 52, 53
Albright, William F., 53
Albright Institute, 48
Alexander Robertson Professorship, Glasgow University, 95
Alexander the Great, 2
Algeria, 26, 38
Ali, Muhammed, 64
Alinsky, Saul, 54
All Saints Episcopal Church, Pasadena, 71
American Academy of Religion, 93
American School of Oriental Research (Albright Institute), 53
Ancient Biblical Manuscript Center (ABMC), 86–89, 98
Anderson, Berhard W.,
Anderson, Marian, 62
Anti-intellectualism, 1, 2, 22, 105
Anti-science, 92
Anti-war, 103
Anti-racism, 103
Anti-environmentalism, 105
Apartheid, 3, 6, 8, 10, 15, 18, 21–22, 32, 35, 54, 68–69, 90, 99
Aristotle, 97
Ashe, Arthur, 85
Auburn Theological Seminary, 65, 72

Bailey, Lloyd, 65
Balmer, Randall, 80
Barnard College, 64
Barthélemy, Fr. Jean-Dominique, 67, 95

Bechtel, Elizabeth Hay, 50, 55, 58, 59, 86–89
Bechtel, Kenneth, 50
Bedford Styvesant, Brooklyn, 76–77, 102
Beirut, 51, 59
Belgium, 25
Bellagio, Italy, 89, 94
Belmont Methodist Church, Nashville, 21–22
Bennett, John, 56, 62, 65-66, 72
Berrigan, Daniel, 4, 80, 99
Berrigan, Philip, 4, 80, 99
Biblia Hebraica Quinta, 67
Biblical criticism, 61
Black Codes, 14
Botha, Piet, 69
Brower, Dean Gerald, 50
Brown vs. Board of Education, 33
Brown, Raymond E., 72
Bulletin of the American Schools of Oriental Research, 53
Bush, George W., 108, 112, 113

Calvary Methodist Episcopal Church, South, 14–15
Calvin, John, 5, 96
Campbell, Rev. Ernest, 63, 74–75
Capetown, 69, 71, 90
Carnet de Famille, 38
Carr, David M., 96
Cave 11 Psalms Scroll, 52, 86
Christian Activities Council, 27–28
Church of Scotland, 95–96
Civil Rights Act (1964), 16, 91, 98